Paolo Hewitt grew up in care ~~~~~~~~~~
and 70s, an experience he chro~~~~~ ~~
memoir, *The Looked After Kid*. He moved to London
in 1980 to become a music journalist and worked for
Melody Maker and *NME*. In the early 1990s Paolo
gave up full-time journalism to write his first novel,
Heaven's Promise. He has since written biographies of
The Jam, The Small Faces, Oasis and Steve Marriott.
He lives in London.

PAUL WELLER

THE CHANGING MAN

Paolo Hewitt

CORGI BOOKS

TRANSWORLD PUBLISHERS
61–63 Uxbridge Road, London W5 5SA
A Random House Group Company
www.rbooks.co.uk

THE CHANGING MAN
A CORGI BOOK: 9780552156097

First published in Great Britain
in 2007 by Bantam Press
a division of Transworld Publishers
Corgi edition published 2008

The author and publisher are grateful to Paul Drew for permission to
reproduce his poem 'Entertainment' from *Mixed Up, Shook Up*, copyright ©
1979, published by Riot Stories, London 1979.

This book is a work of non-fiction.

A CIP catalogue record for this book
is available from the British Library.

Addresses for Random House Group Ltd companies outside the UK
can be found at: www.randomhouse.co.uk
The Random House Group Ltd Reg. No. 954009

The Random House Group Limited supports The Forest Stewardship Council
(FSC), the leading international forest certification organisation. All our titles
that are printed on Greenpeace approved FSC certified paper carry the FSC
logo. Our paper procurement policy can be found at
www.rbooks.co.uk/environment

Typeset in 11.5/15pt Sabon by
Falcon Oast Graphic Art Ltd.

Printed in the UK by CPI Cox & Wyman, Reading, RG1 8EX.

6 8 10 9 7

Every effort has been made to obtain the necessary permissions with reference
to copyright material, both illustrative and quoted. We apologize for any
omissions in this respect and will be pleased to make the appropriate
acknowledgements in any future edition.

'Beauty is truth, truth beauty, – that is all
Ye know on earth, and all ye need to know.'

John Keats

Every successful writer needs a sliver of ice in
their heart.

Graham Greene

Ah, you didn't think that I wouldn't salute you, little one, the woman who made me truly understand the meaning and the power of unconditional love? Love always, always love.

Contents

ACKNOWLEDGEMENTS

I spent many months in the British Library going through interviews conducted with Paul Weller. Sources I have used include *New Musical Express*, *Melody Maker*, *Record Mirror*, *Sounds*, *Mojo* and *Uncut*. Thank you to the patient staff in that building, as well as in Colindale.

Molte grazie to: Don Martino, Amanda and Jo Jo, running molasses out of Ally Pally way; to Toby Jones operating out of Shreveport and Stockwell; to Marco Nelson and his Occasional String Band operating down South; to the other Marco operating *Il Pappagone* on the Stroud Green Road; to Kevin Rowland operating over East; to Linda, Niamh and Clara Taylor-Hughes, taking care of Southgate; to Mark Powell covering Soho; to Iain Munn running Dundee; to all the Arifs taking care of Oxford, Birmingham and deep South, especially Anaia; to George and Jenny bravely operating near the eye of the hurricane; to Frankie, Peter and Katie taking care of Balcome; to Nina, Susie, Tanya, Nick and Stu covering Somerset way; and to Paul and Vicki Hallam looking after Surrey. I also want to single out Emma Musgrave, Sheila Lee, Sam Jones and the book's editor, Doug

Young. *Molte grazie*. My biggest thanks go to David Luxton who came to me with the idea for this book and then became my agent, a turn of events which I am very grateful for.

I dedicate this book to Roberto and Michelle Howard, to Johnny C., Inky and Sterling, to Giovanni Taylor, to you Bax, but especially to you, Mr Wells of Forest Row.

INTRODUCTION

Between the years 1980 and 2006, Paul Weller was my closest friend. He no longer holds that position, and that is fine. People come together, people change, people move on. Such is the way of those who guide us from above.

During the time I was close to him, Paul would often say prior to a press interview, in that exasperated tone of his I got to know so well, 'I don't know why they ask me all these questions. It's all there in the songs if they bothered to look.' This book takes Paul at his word and seeks to draw out both the man and his story through his songwriting. Selecting those songs which I think are of interest, I have sought to examine his words to see what they reveal of him and his complex character. I have also in some places tried to guide the reader to those songs which I feel have been neglected over the years. Forgive me for my presumptuousness.

Paul Weller has been writing songs for over thirty years now. Within that quite sizeable body of work he has placed numerous clues and confessions as to his true nature. This is because music is the only place where he finds full expression. 'I have always felt the need to write,' he said in May 2000. 'There's something about writing that makes me feel complete and whole as a person. It's almost like my whole worth in life hangs around whether I can write these songs or not and whether they are going to impress me enough to make me play them to you and impress you.'

In public and in private, Paul is heavily guarded, careful of revelation. He has always been this way. In December 1977, *Sounds* writer Chas De Whalley noted of him, 'His words are awkward and his tone is dry. In fact, his lack of recognisable rhetoric and his taciturn conversation might tempt many to pigeon hole this nineteen year old as hopelessly inarticulate . . .' It is an observation that applies to this day, one that echoes down the years, and one that, as psychologist Anthony Storr noted, would seem to be common to all creative people. In his 1972 book *The Dynamics of Creation*, Storr wrote, 'Great artists are seldom great talkers.' He later added, 'This needful secrecy, however, means that creative people very often reveal less of themselves in company than ordinary people.'

This is certainly true of Paul. Verbal communication is simply not his strength. Instead, throughout his career, he has displayed an incessant drive to create and to improve. This impulse has produced a staggering amount of songs, nearly five hundred at last count. Seventeen studio albums have emerged, sixty-seven hit singles have been created. Five live albums, countless compilations, three greatest hits – the list rolls on. Even his most virulent critics have had to acknowledge the man's staying power. 'I may not like his music at all,' wrote *Uncut* editor Allan Jones in February 2006, 'but I have to hand it to him for staying the course.'

Paul maintains incredibly high standards. It is of paramount importance to him that he feels he is moving forward artistically, even if others disagree. Every song has to be better than the last one, every album a progression. He told *Vox* magazine in 1996 – and this after launching one of the great comebacks in recent musical history, selling a million copies of his *Stanley Road* album – 'I can't rest, I am always trying to prove myself.' In private, he often explained his philosophy to me. 'You are only as good as your last album, your last gig,' he would state. 'That's why you spend your whole time looking for that one line, that one melody that's going to kick you off. You never get a day off in this job. That's what people never realize.'

Weller remains a restless musician, always looking for new avenues of musical expression, never sticking to the one songwriting style (as he came close to doing in The Jam) but rather looking to assimilate a range of influences into his work. Just a cursory glance at his song list reveals his success at doing so. There is the power punk of In The City, the rich beauty of It's A Very Deep Sea (Diving), the sublime acoustic beauty of Wild Wood, the charged rush of The Changing Man, the spirituality of the hymn-like Wings Of Speed, to mention but five. In 1983 he experimented with jazz, in 1988 classical music, and the year after that Acid House music. With his seventh solo album, *As Is Now*, made at the age of forty-seven, Weller created a work that stylistically refused to stand still. Consider the album's last three songs: Roll On Summer is a lovely acoustic song, a mid tempo paean to the joys of summer; Bring Back The Funk a clever mix of falsetto vocal and funk music; and the final song, The Pebble And The Boy, a rich, mature, piano-led ballad that strikes deep.

Paul Weller is a class songwriter, but he is not a genius. Genius creates brand-new worlds, brand-new horizons. It finds totally new ways of expression, brings a hidden side of the world back to its people. Weller's music is not genius-like; it has too many echoes of others within it. Yet his songwriting remains at a very high standard, and his desire constantly to push himself, I believe, makes Paul Weller unique in British music.

This is a man who steadfastly refuses the easy route. He could, like others, make the same album every year, play the same games. Instead, as time goes by, he has raised the standard of both his songwriting and his live performances. As much as he can, Weller tries to write that which will satisfy him ten years hence. Meanwhile, his live shows, increasingly noted for their energy and ferocity, easily see the back of two hours.

There are reasons for this manic activity. For Paul Weller, fading away into mellowness is a horror to be avoided at all costs. In 1983, at the age of twenty-five, he had already identified it as the enemy, telling *Smash Hits*, 'I don't want to mellow out, I want to become more direct.' Fourteen years later, when Stuart Bailie at the *NME* wrote that a couple of songs on Paul's album *Heavy Soul* were 'Claptonesque', you could hear the explosion for miles around. Weller phoned Bailie at the *NME* offices and berated him. For Paul, to become laid back is an utter betrayal of the energy forces of life. To ease up is to invite the tolling of your final bell. 'I've still got edge in my music,' he said in 1995, 'and hopefully always will have. And if my music got as laid back as Eric Clapton's, I'd pack it in . . . or shoot myself.'

There is another reason for Paul's obsessional need to keep his music young: it keeps him relevant. For most of his life, since his third album, *All Mod Cons*, he has been at the centre of contemporary musical debate. His opinions on music are often sought. In 1983, What does he think of Wham!? In 1995, What does he think of Oasis? In 2005, What does he think of The Libertines? Paul likes this position, likes it a lot. It means he is being taken seriously. It wouldn't be enough for the man to operate like The Stones, as a huge money-making machine with no one caring about his views. For Weller, being taken seriously is a very serious matter. It was why he split from The Jam at such an early age. Had he stayed, personally and artistically he would have died a slow and horrible death – a fact lost on a lot of people.

Yet in recent years Weller has begun to question this vocation of his. 'I don't know if I'd like to live the rest of my life like this,' he said in May 2000, 'where my whole being is bound up in writing a song. I would like to find my own self value, my own self-worth in things outside of coming up with another song.' It is a typical Paul quote, drawn from a man forever questioning himself. The great composer Aaron Copland asked the very same thing back in 1950 in his series of lectures entitled *Music and Imagination*. 'The serious composer who thinks about his art,' Copland stated, 'will sooner or later have occasion to ask himself, why is it so important to my own psyche that I compose music? What makes it seem so absolutely necessary so that every other daily activity, by comparison, is of lesser significance?' Copland offered two answers to this question. The artist, he first argued, needed his art for self-expression; without it there would be no outlet for the composer's numerous and varied emotions. Secondly, for a musician, the act of creation is inextricably tied up in the search for self-knowledge. 'I must create,' Copland said, 'in order to know myself, and since self-knowledge is a never-ending search, each new work is only a part answer to the question, who am I?'

All this is true of Weller. His search for self-knowledge through music has resulted in three very distinct Paul Wellers emerging. There is the uptight, sombre youth who pushed The Jam forward with such passion and rigid righteousness. There is the relaxed, expansive man of The Style Council who revelled in his changing character and developing musicality. And then there is the solo artist who began his career asking who and what am I, and then went on to explore various personal obsessions and themes in his songs and to take a much more 'rock' star position.

Another insight of Copland's into the creative musician is worth noting: 'He is oppressed by excessively powerful instinctual needs. He desires to win honour, power, wealth, fame and the love of women; but he lacks the means for achieving these satisfactions. Consequently, like any other unsatisfied men, he turns away from reality and transfers all his interests and libido too, to the wishful construction of his life of phantasy . . .' As Paul discovered, to his increasing pleasure, the music business is the perfect environment in which to suspend reality. 'You can behave terribly badly in this job and get away with it,' he noted in 1995. That is because the artist is granted special status, diplomatic immunity. As long as success is his companion, the artist is refused nothing, excused everything. Low record sales? Fault of the record company for not getting behind the album, never the album itself. A bad gig? Fault of the audience. Bad ticket sales? Fault of the promoter. And so on.

The music business has given Paul his every freedom,

although he has always seen through its façade, especially the Paul who drove The Jam forward and wrote All Mod Cons and To Be Someone, two of the best songs about fame and the fickle nature of the music business. 'Four years ago,' he noted in 1995, 'I couldn't get arrested. Now it's people saying, great, always liked your stuff. That's the nature of this business, and once you understand it, you get on with it. It is quite simple – you can't trust it.'

Throughout his career, Weller's musical aim has remained constant: to write great songs. For Weller, the song is all. 'Melody is very important to me,' he said in 1980. 'It's the best way to communicate. A good melody is a plane or a form of communication which everyone can relate to.' Although he has veered into various areas of experimentation, he has never been interested in breaking musical barriers or establishing fresh musical territory (although he respects many who do, especially within the field of jazz). No, what Weller has always wanted is to give to people the same magic bands had given to him as a little boy growing up in Woking. The work of groups such as The Beatles, The Kinks, The Beach Boys and The Small Faces, the records of Motown and Stax, the music of Jamaica, all had a profound effect on him as he grew up. He can still remember the emotions evoked in him the day he first heard Strawberry Fields by The Beatles. 'That line in Strawberry Fields,' he stated in 1996, ' "no one I know is in my tree", meant something to me even at that age.' His job, as he saw it, was to pass on that very same magic to the world at large.

It is no secret or surprise, then, that his musical template is based on sixties principles. This, for him, is *the* great era of pop, the magical time when pop music kept evolving in all kinds of wondrous ways, when the charts were dominated by young, well-dressed bands singing great three-minute pop songs. This is how Paul has seen himself from the outset: advancing pop, doing so in smart attire, and gaining commercial success. He wanted the acclaim *and* the moolah. He often said to me, 'What's the point of making a record no one will hear?'

Image is vital to this process, a fact that Paul picked up very early on. I recall lending him a tape of a 1969 Nina Simone concert, broadcast from Elstree Studios, an intimate affair with a young British audience crowded around her. 'Brilliant,' Paul said, 'I'd love to do a gig like that, everyone in the audience really well dressed.' A smart image was of paramount importance, and this partly accounts for his virulent hatred of seventies contemporary music. 'I detested those groups such as Slade,' he stated in 1995, '*detested* them.' He later added, 'It is incredible now to think of the amount of success that Gary Glitter achieved for someone fat and middle-aged.'

To Paul, such music reeked of calculation, evoked memories of that dreaded beast show business, which also ran on similar principles. That's because Paul grew up in a time when show business, or light entertainment, was the mainstream. The insipid nature of the music, the false smiles and hairpieces, the glitzy surroundings, the age of the performers (too old), infuriated him – as did the over-the-top attire of Slade, the knowing clothes of Roxy Music, the fur and glitter of Bolan. He remains the only musician of his generation not to have been seriously influenced by the work of David Bowie. (In the mid 1990s, Paul started hanging out with the Primal Screams and Oasises of the world. One night, a kind of supergroup idea was mooted, playing pubs in summertime. Paul was all in favour until the idea of covering a Mott The Hoople song was put forward. 'Mott The Hoople? Fucking joking, aintcha?' was his terse reply to that idea.)

Weller's musical tastes in the 1970s were mainly located in ska and soul, the music of choice for all the young suedeheads. 'If you were a skinhead or a suedehead,' he said in 1995, 'you listened to soul or reggae.'

Yet his musical impulses were not to be denied. He had dreamt of being a pop star at ten, been given his first guitar at twelve, was competent by fourteen. The first time seventies rock music had a real effect on Paul was *not*, as has often been stated, in 1976 when he saw The Pistols at the Lyceum, but a year earlier, when he saw Dr Feelgood, that blistering r'n'b band, at Guildford Civic Hall. That concert had a huge impact on Paul, changing his guitar style and his band's look in just one stroke. (The early Jam image of 1976–77 was pure Dr Feelgood, with the black suits and white shirts, whilst musically the influence can still be heard today:

check the opening riffs to his songs Blink And You'll Miss It and From The Floorboards Up from his last album.)

The Pistols show at the Lyceum is important, though, as this was the first time Paul had witnessed a band of his own age playing music on stage. 'They had short hair, straight trousers, they didn't have beards,' he told *Mojo* magazine. 'It made a difference to me.' (Note how he homed in straight away on the band's image, not the music.) The Pistols gave Paul ideas, inspiration. Within a year he had his first hit single. Few could have prophesied then that this callow, shy teenager from the sticks would outlast and outwrite all his contemporaries. But he did. He would make The Jam the most popular band in the United Kingdom, with one of the most fanatical followings ever seen. Then, at the height of their success, he would make what the writer Tony Parsons called the 'bravest decision by a musician since Stevie Wonder and Marvin Gaye single-handedly challenged Motown', and split The Jam. He then formed The Style Council and embarked on an idiosyncratic musical adventure that divided many as to its worth. In this decade alone, jazz, blues, Latin, soul, Northern Soul, funk, hip hop and Acid House were all enthusiastically investigated and brought into his work. In the 1990s, late sixties and seventies rock music – Traffic and Neil Young being prime examples – were added to the list.

Part of Weller's skill is his ability to assimilate these influences into his work and then go about creating something fresh. Like every other songwriter, he also has no compulsion about lifting ideas from anywhere and everywhere – book titles (Absolute Beginners), song titles (You Do Something To Me), even house names (Wild Wood). He felt little guilt in doing so because he had known from an early age that this was what the big boys did. The Beatles did, Dylan did, Townshend did, everyone. So why not he? The difference was that when Weller plundered he did so in a righteous manner. He didn't just take from others and leave it at that. He took the musical booty and then transmuted it into his own. As he coolly explained in 1980, 'I do it all the time, but that's because I love music. Whatever I listen to I probably use, if I like it – whether consciously or subconsciously. It is what it is there for. Let's not be too precious about it. It is only somebody's bleedin' chords and melodies you've used, but it is *how* you use them and what you put into them that counts.'

Paul quickly grasped that in music, little is original. He discovered this fact early by carefully studying bands and building up a huge music collection. Records are so precious for Weller. I remember one night in the 1980s, after yet another argument with his then girlfriend Gill Price, I had to accompany Paul home in a cab. On the journey back to his flat, Paul wasn't at all worried about appeasing her; he just desperately wanted to make sure she left his collection of precious Small Faces import singles alone.

Music is his lifeblood, the engine of his life. He has an almost encyclopaedic knowledge of his craft. He adored musical biographies, soaked them up by the dozen. When my biography of The Small Faces lead singer Steve Marriott, *All Too Beautiful*, was published I sent him a copy, then settled back and waited for the inevitable phone call. Sure enough, it came through two days later. 'Good book, but "Good Loving" wasn't by The Rascals,' he curtly told me. 'The original was by The Olympics. Behave. Catch you later.' Then the phone went dead. When he worked with Paul McCartney on the War Child single, he told the Beatle's daughter Stella that her dad had chipped his front tooth in a moped accident in 1966. Stella looked at him in a kind of horrified wonder. 'You know more about my father than I do,' she said.

He met many of his heroes. McCartney and Ray Davies, for example, have both been told *exactly* what they mean to him. When I interviewed another of his heroes, Steve Marriott, in 1984, I asked Paul along, but he refused to attend. He didn't want reality to break his dream of the man. Instead, he gave me two questions to ask him. One was, why don't you make a blistering r'n'b record like you used to do? Marriott replied succinctly, 'Why don't you come to a gig, you cunt?'

Paul liked that reply, liked it a lot.

Paul Weller's musical career is inextricably bound up in the British class system. For many, Paul is a true working-class hero, the no-nonsense geezer who made it but did so on his terms. Paul has never wavered from his convictions. He will stand up to anyone, be it his audience, his critics, even his bosses (his run-in with David Munns over the release of the last Style Council album has entered folklore). His fans adore him for this non-compromising stance. I recall walking down the road with him in Covent Garden once, 'having a mooch around' as we used to call it, and a builder in front of us suddenly glancing over his shoulder and blurting out, 'Fuck me, it's the King of England.' He wasn't the only one who thought so. To this day, Paul Weller inspires such great devotion from people that many dress like him, talk like him.

Weller is extremely proud to be working class. He hangs on to his roots with a vice-like grip. When somebody recently suggested that given his lifestyle and money he was now middle class, again, you could hear the explosion for miles around. 'Fucking middle class?' he ranted. 'I'll never be fucking middle class.'

And he was right, of course. Class is about attitude, not money. Despite all the trappings his work has given him – the beautiful house, the private schools, the cleaners, the nannies – Paul has remained resolutely working class. He changes for no one. How can he? After all, the Mod culture he adores so much is resolutely British and working class.

'I'll always be a Mod,' he told Jonathan Ross once. 'They will bury me a Mod.' In 1995, he explained, 'In the sixties and seventies, any spare money went on clothes and records. That's the culture we created.' As we already know, records and clothes are of deep importance to Paul. The journalist Chris Sullivan once asked him to nominate his five favourite pieces of clothing for a newspaper article. 'But I couldn't do it,' he told me. 'It is just too personal for that stuff to be made public.'

Paul's personal style constantly and organically developed. It enraged him when journalists accused him of changing images, *à la* Bowie. He was never that calculated, he firmly stated, he was just following his tastes, and whether he made records or not, he would keep on doing so. Paul experimented with all kinds of looks, within the large Modernist framework. There was the uptight Carnaby Street/Marriott Mod of the seventies, the European Modernist of the eighties with dashes of casual fashion thrown in, the more colourful spiritual Mod of the nineties, the designer-led Mod of today.

What, then, did his clothes say about his character, apart from an obvious desire to be one up on everyone else?

In the recent BBC2 film on his career, *Into Tomorrow*, Paul's long-time drummer Steve White referred to Paul as 'a lovely bunch of fellas'. One would have to take issue with the word 'lovely', though. Paul is certainly a bunch of fellas, but he is far too complex a man for one adjective to do all the work. Paul Weller is a storm of complexes, a man of wide moods, riven with contradictions, impossible to predict. He feels life deeply. When obsession grips, it grips hard, and he has to follow its call, no matter the consequence. He questions all that comes into his life, examines everything from every angle. 'Maybe I take life too seriously,' he once noted, 'but I see a depth in things. That's why I feel I have got a heavy soul.' Like all seekers of the truth, this trait makes him a real pain in the arse, and a man of great vision. He also has a streak of anger in him that stays close to the surface, an anger that colours his work, and transmits itself to anyone around him. As *Melody Maker* writer Adam Sweeting once perceptively noted of Paul, 'He often appears to be holding a large abstract grudge against something that hasn't quite happened yet.'

He was born on 25 May 1958. Others born around that time of year include Bob Dylan, Stevie Wonder and Pete Townshend. His sign is Gemini, the sign of the twins. That is appropriate. Paul really does have an angel on one shoulder and a gargoyle on the other; in my experience, the day often depended on who got the first word in. It is a condition not made better by his devastating mood changes. He was the one person in my life I was always wary of ringing up. You never knew which Paul would come to the phone. It might be happy Paul, angry Paul, depressed Paul. You just had no way of knowing. It made him a minefield to negotiate.

Of course, Paul could be lovely and generous and thoughtful and kind and warm and funny, too. He also had, contrary to public belief, a wicked sense of humour – sharp, often self-deprecating. 'Do you like being called The Modfather?' a *Daily Mirror* writer asked him recently. 'Look at it this way,' he replied, 'it's better than being called a cunt.' When rehearsing his song Brushed, just prior to recording, Paul asked the band if they thought the song's riff was too much like a Noel Gallagher song. A couple of people hummed and hawed until Paul went, 'Oh fuck it, Noel's in America today, he'll never know,' and started playing again. I once ran into some trouble with the law. Paul told me not to worry. 'After all,' he pointed out with a cheeky grin, 'don't all great writers go to prison at some point in their lives?'

Paul has a very good heart beating away inside him. He showed a great generosity of spirit when the mood took him. Yet he could also be mean, aggressive, bullying, incredibly selfish, highly intolerant, and very thoughtless. He has a terrible tongue, which he uses as a defence mechanism. Attack first, ask questions later, is the philosophy. I know of two people who now refuse to go backstage to see him, so wary are they of his verbal lashings. 'I start off from the point that people don't like me,' he once said. 'that way it can only get better.' It's a strange position to take. Most people adopt the reverse attitude. Was Paul aware of these shortcomings? Absolutely, otherwise he couldn't have written so many songs with his failings as their subject.

Meg Matthews, Noel Gallagher's first wife, often said to me, 'Why is it that every time I hear a Paul Weller record, he is always saying sorry?' 'Well,' I'd reply, 'he does get up to quite a lot, that boy . . .'

Certainly in his younger days there was a very real rest-lessness and discontent about Paul. Nothing seemed to satisfy him, there was no inner peace. Many were the times you would walk away from an evening with him and think, 'He has it all, the success, the money, the house, the woman, and still he moans.' It was the arrival of children and the realization, after many years, of the strength of his talent that brought him a measure of inner peace.

Paul is a very dominant, forceful character. This makes him a real control freak and, according to his own testimony, he imposes himself on the assembled, loves to control situations. When he wants to get his case across, he does so with great gusto. He is a bag of nerves, a constant mover, but he sees himself as the leader in every situation, 'very difficult to live with', as he admitted in May 2000. 'I'm a bit moody. One day I am happy, half an hour later I am unhappy. I am aware of it, but that's just the way I am.' Later, he told *Word* magazine, 'My girlfriend said to me the other day, "You're psychotic." Which is possible.' His mood swings with such intensity that people tend to keep their distance – which is fine by Paul. His artistic temperament demands that he can only allow you so far into his domain. These mood shifts, from happiness to anger for example, make his character one of extreme contradictions. This is a man who speaks of music as his religion, a sacred force that has to be respected at all times. Yet five of his major songs have been sanctioned for adverts to promote the National

Lottery, Ribena, Adidas and Clarks shoes, and the English Tourist Board. He often refers to the importance of family and friends, yet neglected to acknowledge either in his Lifetime Achievement Award speech at the Brit Awards in 2006. He speaks of his huge self-respect and pride, but would drink himself into a dribbling wreck of a man. He is the Modernist who rails against the technology that makes the world modern. 'And if that makes me sound like a grumpy old man,' he said just last year, 'I don't care.'

Personally, I saw in Paul a complex mix of characteristics that are uniquely English and totally disparate. Paul was Alex, the violent droogie from the film *A Clockwork Orange*, mixed with Shelley, the Romantic poet. He was William Blake and Oliver Reed, combined. A mystic ruffian, a hooligan with the eye of a poet and the tongue of a builder. In Paul, angry John Lennon met peaceful Nick Drake, via Joe Orton and George Orwell. It was an intriguing mix. He spent a weekend in Rome last year. How was it? I asked him when he got back. 'Weird,' he replied. 'I kept seeing flashes of red everywhere.'

Some days he would argue that all his wealth and good fortune were down to him alone and his hard work; other times he would make reference to his 'charmed life'. Nature speaks deeply to him. He believes in a higher power, feels that in the scheme of things he has been placed on this earth to play music. He is a huge believer in sending signals out into the world. I recall him telling how in New York once he was missing his son Nathaniel so much he played the song he had written for him, Moon On Your Pyjamas, at a radio show so as to connect to him. Still, 'I get these insecurities,' he told *Mojo* magazine, 'or a sense of failure, or the idea that I am not living up to what I want to get to. Other times, I walk off the stage at Phoenix or T in the Park and I know exactly what I am doing and why I am here.'

His uncontrollable anger could rush out in a stream of raw invective. He has asked me outside for a fight at least three times, once because I spoke in favour of the internet. He has a brooding presence which fills the room to such an uncomfortable level that people are forced into silence. Sometimes it was hard for me to believe that this was the man who wrote English Rose, The Start Of Forever, You Who Bring Joy; the man who once danced through a field of poppies; the man who made me stay up till five in the morning so that he could show me the sun clash with clouds in a dramatic Oxford sky; the man who would give me a flower with love, to take home, or the man who once phoned me to play the sound of the Mediterranean Sea into my answering machine.

Friendship with Paul was a double-edged sword, as is any relationship with a high-profile figure. Many people would sneer at me and say, 'You just want to be Paul Weller.' Which I never did. Many people would then sneer again and say, 'You're just jealous of him.' Which I never was. His fame and riches never interested me. The complexities of his moods and the unhappiness it brought him actually elicited sympathy in me. He may be rich and famous, but there is a cost. I doubt that there has been one close relationship in his life in which he has not seriously upset the person in question. His arrogance also makes demands: that he never apologize, that he is always in control of a relationship. I would not swap roles with him for all the shoes in Italy.

The only spark of jealousy I ever felt towards Paul was to do with his height. Whatever he wore, the man always looked good. That was it.

Paul is highly self-centred – a prerequisite of all song writers. Everything has to relate to him. When Paul once urged me to have a child, he did so 'because it would make *me* really happy'. If I moaned about something, his immediate response was always, well, what about me? What about what *I* have to go through? I grumbled to his mum once about an important message Paul had completely forgotten to give me. 'Yeah, but you know what he's like, love,' she replied. 'He's too busy thinking about a new shirt or a new pair of shoes.' If I ever criticized or pulled Paul up on something, he never conceded that I might have a point. Instead, he turned the tables: 'Well, what about you? You do that as well.'

Many people saw my relationship with Paul as a glamour-filled fun escapade. Much of it was, and I wouldn't swap that past for the world. But being Paul Weller is not an easy occupation. This is a man who basically goes to bed not knowing quite who he will be when he wakes the next day. It is the journey between these various states of being that this book seeks to examine. In the process I hope it will reveal the man, this one-off man, responsible for some remarkable music, for it is also the journey into the heart of a true songwriter whose talent we should cherish. But he remains a man who, like tomorrow's dawn light, will always be a little out of the reach of the rest of us.

Paolo Hewitt
London, 2007

ONE

In The City (*In The City*, 1977)

Paul, Woking, London, Punk and Youth Obsession

So where did I first meet this man who would have such an impact on my life, a man a mutual friend once memorably described as 'an enigma rolled up in a ten-bob note'? In Woking, of course, in a cheap high-street shoe shop, where I worked Saturdays and holidays.

On the day we met, my good *amico* Enzo Esposito had been hanging out with Paul, the pair of them driving round Woking on Paul's scooter. Both were musicians. Paul played in a band called The Jam, Enzo was in an outfit called Squire. They paid me a visit at the shop.

It was 1975, the year of the soul boy, of David Bowie's *Young Americans* album, of flared trousers, platform shoes and tank tops. Paul stood in front of me in a green parka, black Sta-prest trousers, white socks, button-down shirt and loafer shoes. He looked so back-dated it was startling, a man truly out of time.

Paul nodded at me, didn't say a word the whole time he and Enzo were there. But the meet did mean that if he saw me around Woking he would pull over on his scooter and have a brief chat. You're Enzo's mate, aintcha? (Yes.) You seen Enzo? (Yes.) Is he OK? (Yes.) How's his band Squire doing? (Not so well. They are still playing bad Status Quo covers.) OK then, see ya.

Of course, I knew about Paul's band, The Jam, but it was impossible to see them play. Although they had a residency at a local club called Michael's, the band performed upstairs, in the members-only section. Us young leaves of Woking were not allowed in. However, thanks to a very loud Australian girl tourist that Vic Falsetta, another Italiano *amico* of mine, and I met in the Wheatsheaf pub one night, we managed to gain entry.

At the time, The Jam were a five-piece, playing a lot of r'n'b covers, Smokey Robinson especially, and I remember thinking how very slick, how very professional they were. A year later, their name, which I actively hated, was suddenly on everyone's lips. EMI Records were showing some interest. The buzz in Woking was palpable. Were there actual stars in our midst, in Woking? Impossible. The buzz died down and the long hot summer of 1976 kicked in.

Like Paul, I was an avid *NME* reader, so I knew all about the developing punk scene in London. I didn't realize that The Jam had now dropped their soulful prettiness and were now purveyors of punk-energized r'n'b, however – until April 1977, the month when everyone suddenly realized that something serious was going on with The Jam. The 11 April issue of the *NME* arrived in Woking as usual on a Thursday afternoon. Paul Weller, Bruce Foxton and Rick Buckler were on the cover. I had been reading the *NME* since I was fourteen and I was mightily impressed. It meant this band was being taken very seriously. I read the interview three times, and was left puzzled and bemused by Weller's comments on politics (pro Tory) and the royal family (pro the Queen).

That night I turned on *Top of the Pops* and there they were performing the song in question, In The City. I bought the record the very next morning, played it several times in the afternoon, and in the evening went to meet friends, at the Cotteridge pub in Woking. By chance, I was early. I walked in, went up to the bar, glanced round and froze. Who should be sitting behind me at an empty table, on his own, chewing his nails, smoking furiously, wearing a black Harrington and bright red cords with a scowl the size of Woking across his face?

Immediately I turned back to the bar, hoping Paul Weller hadn't seen me.

This was the thinking. If I said hello and sat with him, he might think I was only doing so because he had been on TV the night before. Didn't want that. I was into punk, and admiring pop stars was strictly off the agenda. But if I didn't say hello, he might think I saw him as a dreaded pop star. Didn't want that, either. (Punk's rules and regulations certainly introduced a lot of complexities into seventies teenage life.)

As I weighed up my options, Paul unexpectedly came to the bar and solved my problem.

'You're Enzo's mate, aintcha?'

Weller was waiting on friends as well. We sat down at the table, spoke for a few minutes before people began arriving. The conversation, as I recall it, was about *NME* writers, a breed I was obsessed with at the time.

'You have met Tony Parsons? Fucking hell.'

'Yeah, he and Julie Burchill took me down to Twickenham to meet Townshend.'

'You've met Julie Burchill? Fucking hell. And they took you to meet Pete Townshend?'

'Yeah.'

Paul took a drag on his ciggy, nodded his head calmly. He was already nonchalant, worldly-wise. To me, it felt as if he lived in a galaxy it would take me a lifetime to reach.

'What about Charles Shaar Murray? Nick Kent?' I asked.

'Nah, haven't met them, although Tony Parsons told me there was a lot of office politics going on, between the punk writers and the others.'

For me, this was glamour. Paul Weller, privy to *NME* office politics, hanging out with writers I read avidly every week. Amazing. Paul was a massive *NME* reader as well, but he kept quiet on the subject. He often kept a lot of his enthusiasms under wraps – no doubt a lesson learnt from his poker-playing father. Never show your cards early; always keep them tight to your chest.

Friends arrived, and on that boisterous teenage night all of us drank to excess. A couple of memories stick. I recall Paul trying to light the back of the jacket of the bar owner every time the old man wobbled by. I also clearly remember him ripping the cords he had on, from the bottom up, leaving his legs showing.

The next time I saw Paul was at the Wheatsheaf. I had started writing for a fanzine, and wanted to interview him. It was impossible to ask him this in public, so I waited for a chance. When he slid off to the toilets, I made my move. I followed him in.

'All right?'

'All right?'

Silence. Splashing.

'Yeah, look, I'm writing for this fanzine . . .'

'That's good.'

'Just wanted to know if, like, I could interview ya.'

I presumed he would say yes. It was de rigueur then not to turn down fanzine requests. To do so was to suggest you were getting above your station – another punk no-no. Naturally, Weller shot me down in a flash.

'Nah, not interested, mate. Sick of fucking interviews. Why don't you do something on reggae instead? That would be really good.'

This was typical Paul, bullish, uncaring one minute, encouraging and thoughtful the next.

I didn't see Paul again until late 1977, just prior to the

release of the album *The Modern World* (see Thick As Thieves).

What, then, of this debut single? In The City is a typical Weller composition in that it borrows from another source, in this case the Pete Townshend composition and B side to the 1966 Who single Happy Jack, In The City, from which Paul takes the chorus vocal line and title, and then takes it somewhere else. The result is a song that was key to the band in their early days. They would open shows with it, close shows with it, and play it again as an encore.

Musically, it packs a great riff. Lyrically, the song contains three major themes: police brutality, London and the power of youth. In one line, Paul hopes fervently that the police are never granted the right to kill indiscriminately. This refers to the death in 1976 of amateur boxer Liddle Towers, who died in police custody. Six officers were implicated in his death but no one was ever tried. The coroner's verdict of justifiable homicide led to widespread condemnation and a call for an inquiry. This event infuriated Paul. (In another song, Time For Truth, he states his hope that the six policemen are hanged, and then shouts out Liddle Towers' name.)

In The City is also one of Paul's first homages to London. London had been important to his psyche for years. In my 1983 Jam biography *A Beat Concerto*, Paul's school friend Steve Carver recalls Weller being so besotted by London that he would travel there and literally tape it. For Paul, London was freedom, the promised land, a musical nirvana, the city where The Beatles made all their records, where The Small Faces lived, where The Who smashed guitars, where the Mods dropped pills, where the punk scene was now making itself acutely felt. By comparison, Woking was a prison, a small town cage. 'The actual town,' he said of Woking in May 1995, 'is a dump. London was a special day out. You would go a couple of times a year, which made it even more magical . . . People had a chance to be themselves in London. In Woking, if you had the wrong cut of trousers you'd get your head kicked in.' (See Town Called Malice for further details.) London was the place to be, and in wishing to plant himself there Weller was years ahead of most Woking people, who lacked even the ambition to move up the street.

The true songwriter must have the obsession about him. He is lost otherwise. Weller the teenager took everything ultra seriously. As soon as he had seen The Pistols at the Lyceum, that was it, Paul fixated on the punk movement. It is a trait that has followed him down the years. Countless times I have seen a type of music such as Acid House or contemporary American soul grab him, and suddenly his universe revolves to a new centre. Punk was no different, although it would prove to be a very short-lived obsession.

Enthusiastic as he might have been, Weller was not prepared for the surly, mocking reception he received from punk's inner circle. The Pistols and The Clash were all London boys. They prided themselves on their

London street-smart and they refused to take Weller seriously – the ultimate affront to this proud man. The Jam were boys from the sticks, not worth considering, with their black mohair suits and Moddy haircuts. After all, Mod was a relic, a throwback. No one was wearing Mod clothes in 1977. Neat suits, neat haircuts? Had Mod just reached Woking ten years after the event? How backward could you get? Punk's leading bands were older than The Jam, and far more knowing. Next to The Pistols, or The Clash, Paul seemed like an earnest young boy who wore all the wrong clothes but followed you around like a puppy – hence Weller's bitter line in this song about approaching people who make him look like a fool.

The Jam went on tour with The Clash. Within days, the two bands were locked into argument. Verbal back-biting was heard all over town. (It was this tour that gave birth to The Clash saying, 'Don't worry, it could be worse: you could be in The Jam.') When, in later years, Paul's designer Simon Halfon mentioned his liking of The Clash, Paul's put-down was brief and vicious. 'Fucking liars,' he retorted, although, again the contra-diction – he much admired Joe Strummer and Mick Jones.

To be mocked in this manner badly wounded Paul. To be scorned by these other bands might have been hypo-critical – punk was supposedly whatever you made it to be; it existed to encourage all into action – but it acted as a resounding slap in the face. Still, a valuable lesson had been learnt: everyone was up for sale, everyone had a price. Now, in Weller World, everyone is presumed guilty until proved innocent. Weller's revenge on these bands was of the best kind: he stayed the course as they fell one by one.

In his first major *NME* interview to promote this song – the one I read so avidly on that Thursday afternoon in April 1977 – Paul told Steve Clarke that all this change-the-world stuff was getting too trendy and that he and the boys would be voting Conservative. He also expressed, as he would all that year, his admiration for the hard-working royal family. 'She's the best diplomat we have got,' he said of the Queen. The statements would haunt him to this day. In his defence, he maintained that the expression of such views was a wind-up job, a distancing of himself from his competitors. Lately, he has even been quoted as saying that his record company was to blame, the band and their then press officer hatching this plan down the pub one day.

Whatever the truth, Weller still harbours great bitterness for these times. 'Punk was a con, big business,' he told *Mojo* in 1995. 'We were never accepted. We were always a little outside of the whole punk circle, which was quite elitist, cliquey and art school . . . we weren't hip at all. We came from Woking. We saw things differently . . . I thought punk was the first working-class musical movement in my time. That's how I perceived it and I think that is why The Jam clicked because we made our own scene. What we and our audiences were was more the real spirit of punk.'

The other line of great interest in this song talks 'about

the young idea' – youth was another fixation of Weller's, still is in many respects, as he mourns its passing. I recall him worrying about age constantly (see Time Passes). 'All the bands I love,' he often told me, 'made their great records when they were eighteen, nineteen, and then they turned shit.' The subtext of this observation was, would the same happen to him? It is one of the reasons why he has kept such a vigilant eye on his work.

Paul truly believed that if he didn't make his mark by eighteen, he should consider packing it in, go back to playing music in the pubs and clubs of Surrey. In The City, then, is a milestone record. It gave Weller his first top forty just before he turned nineteen; but more than that, its success gave him the necessary confidence to convince him of the righteousness of his vision.

After The Jam's demise in 1982, the song remained dormant until last year, when Weller dusted it down and gave it two airings. The first was at a London show guesting with Carl Barat's band Dirty Pretty Things. Weller surprised all by launching into this song, with Barat taking the vocals. They did so a second time as part of the BBC's Prom series which featured Paul with several guests at London's Roundhouse venue. On both occasions the forty-eight-year-old Weller wisely decided to leave the vocals to the youngsters.

TWO

Non Stop Dancing (*In The City*, 1977)

Paul and Soul

At the time of this song's release, April 1977, most people believed in a Holy Trinity of punk: The Pistols, The Clash and The Jam. Of late, The Jam's position within punk history has been disregarded, not least by Paul himself. For example, in his book *Punk* Chris Sullivan deliberately makes no mention of The Jam whatsoever, a decision that found favour with Paul. In later years he has become somewhat Stalinist when considering his past. 'I see you were on TV talking crap,' he told me once after I'd been on, discussing The Jam. By then, I knew him well enough to know that whatever idea he had got in his brain would not be dislodged by my truth or reason. What Paul thought at any given time was the only truth. Same with punk. Although an integral part of it, Paul's distaste for the

1977 scene is such that he now wishes to distance himself as far as possible from it, even if that means rewriting the books.

As we have seen, punk was a scene Paul embraced, purely because in his eyes it should have been 'the first working-class musical movement that our generation had had ... that's what I wanted it to be.' Instead, punk mocked Paul. No wonder.

British working-class culture has never had much to do with rock music. Original Mods, for example, held their noses up at bands such as The Beatles and The Stones and their woeful appropriations of American r'n'b music. Punk never reflected the world of true working-class culture that Paul knew, the world of skinheads and suedeheads, brogue shoes and loafers, button-down shirts, scooters, soul music and amphetamine-induced all-night dancing. This was a parallel world, and as his career unfolded, Paul would be instrumental in highlighting it.

Non Stop Dancing celebrates the Northern Soul scene, and it name-checks James Brown, an artist no one was talking about in 1977.

Paul's first experience of Northern Soul came when he attended an all-nighter as a teenager, probably at Bisley Pavilion near Woking, an event still running today. As usual, Paul stood at the back, and observed. 'I am not a dancer and I couldn't really get into it,' he said in 1978. But over the next few years, Northern Soul became increasingly important to Paul. I recall us going to various Northern nights at clubs such as Le

Beat Route, all of us self-consciously dancing on its tiny stage, Paul too.

On the inside sleeve of The Jam's 1982 album *The Gift*, Paul placed a full-size Kevin Cummins picture of a Northern Soul dancer. He also heavily borrowed from the World Column song So Is The Sun for his own Trans Global Express song. Paul's only beef with the music was that constant exposure to it rendered it quite 'samey'. Still, there were records he absolutely adored: Time Will Pass You By by Tobi Legend, That's Enough by Roscoe Robinson, Picture Me Gone by Madeleine Bell, and If I Could Only Be Sure by Nolan Porter, which featured on his covers album *Studio 150*. This was true council-estate culture, an area Paul explored with much success during his Jam days, and which made him a hero to many.

THREE

I Got By In Time (*In The City*, 1977)

Paul and Friendships (Part One)

While the rest of the musical world in 1977 was devoting itself to singing about anarchy and politicians and dole queues, Paul, with typical individuality, wrote a song examining two major relationships from his past.

Paul's lyrics for most of the Jam debut album and its follow-up, *The Modern World*, are pretty dire. Influenced by Clash frontman Joe Strummer and punk, his songs around this time are littered with words such as 'kids', 'streets', 'fools' and 'sounds'. This song is entirely different. Written when he was just eighteen years old, I Got By In Time focuses on his most significant male and female relationships to date, family excepted. He might have got the idea for the song from a Beach Boys tune he loved, entitled Friends: when we first met, I recall him always enthusing about this song. It is a striking artistic move, one hidden by the ferocity of the music and Paul's hurried, sometimes unintelligible vocals. For years, I always believed the song began 'Shop girl I used to know', not 'Saw a girl I used to know'; and I had no idea that the second verse concerned his close mate Steve Brookes.

The song has three verses. The first recalls a girl – Sharon Boxall – Paul went out with when he was fourteen years old. The second verse, as I said, deals with Steve Brookes. The third verse sums up his thoughts on the nature of relationships, the title a clue to his conclusions.

A flash of self-deprecating humour can be found in the first verse: Paul does not recognize the girl's face because at the time he is too busy looking at his own. Sharon Boxall was not Paul's first romantic relationship ('I think I had my first girlfriend when I was thirteen,' he wrote in *Flexipop*, 'all lovey dovey and cuddling') but she was certainly his first serious romance. 'When I was fourteen,' he continued in *Flexipop*, 'I went "steady" with a girl for eight months (she's me cousin now!). [Sharon's father later married Paul's aunt Mary.] My mum and dad thought I was ill because I spent all my time with her and didn't go out playing football with the lads. My parents were dead against it. I didn't get on with them for ages around that time.'

It is strange for me to hear of Paul and his parents, John and Ann, not getting on 'for ages' (see Call Me). From my vantage point, the Wellers were a close-knit family, Italian-like in their devotion, their determination. These were parents who sacrificed much to realize their son's dreams, who poured unconditional love into their children, especially the first born. Why they disliked Sharon remains unknown, although a very educated guess might be that for the first time the apple of their eye was focusing his attention elsewhere, upsetting the rhythm of their lives. As the song states, 'she was the only girl I had ever loved', she was his world, the one he thought he could never live without.

He thought that about Steve Brookes too. There was no way he could have known then that Brookes would one day write a fine, insightful book about their time together. This self-published work, *Keeping the Flame* (1996), is the most valuable document of Paul's character and his emerging songwriting talent at this point in his life. It is also striking how my relationship with Paul followed a similar path to Steve's. There is a meeting, a mutual attraction made through music, promises of eternal friendship, a dispute, and then silence.

Weller met Brookes at Sheerwater Secondary School in November 1972. He was introduced to him by a mutual friend, Roger Pilling. Brookes describes Pilling as tall, prone to waving his arms around and making strange noises. 'Paul obviously liked him because he was so different,' Brookes states. On meeting Brookes, Paul simply grunted and wandered off for a fag. Later, the boys got talking. Both were musicians, and Paul's birthday preceded Brookes' by a day. Paul invited Steve to his house. Brookes writes of 'the warmth and homeliness' he encountered at Stanley Road, how later he was envious of the family closeness, and how he thought Paul at fourteen was 'pretty advanced'.

It was music that truly brought them together. They began to see each other on a regular basis, showing each other what they had learnt on the guitar, swapping techniques, riffs, etc. Their bible was The Beatles song-book. Brookes recalls the two of them spending hours playing Beatles songs. Sometimes, Paul would play him a new composition which obviously had its roots in one of the Lennon and McCartney songs they had been playing. A good example of this would be their song Taking My Love (although when it appeared on The Jam's first album it was credited to Weller only), which according to Brookes started life as 'our own version of a Beatles song called One After 909'.

Indeed, Brookes goes out of his way to establish Paul's deep Beatles obsession. 'He would often look for similarities between himself and McCartney, whether facial or in hairstyles, and he would scan his Beatles monthly magazine to glean other ways of emulating him. He lived and breathed The Beatles and the early sixties and, as McCartney was his idol, he saw it as only fitting that he should play bass in our band when the time came.' The other positions would go to drums, rhythm and lead guitar. 'Name a famous group beginning with the letter B that had that line-up,' Brookes jokes. Again, Paul always followed his impulses. 'He was always immersed in music, and would sometimes get up halfway through a meal and go and try out an idea on the piano under the stairs.'

They played their first gig at school. It was lunchtime. They kept their heads down as they played. When they looked up halfway through a song, they saw the look of wonder on all the girls' faces. Valuable lesson.

More gigs were arranged. The boys played covers, like All I Have To Do Is Dream, Bye Bye Love, Leaving On A Jet Plane, even Green Green Grass Of Home. In pubs and social clubs they drank Scotch and Coke because they knew The Beatles did. One time they played a gig drunk and went into a terrible twenty-minute blues jam. After that, they never drank before performing.

'Our friendship was, by this time, written in stone,' Brookes reveals, 'and the common goal we shared was akin to religious devotion . . . we were really at ease with each other, almost a telepathic understanding.' In his *Flexipop* article, Paul confirmed their closeness. 'We really did love each other then,' he wrote, 'not homosexually, but the kind of PURE love you very rarely get with the opposite sex. We just thought exactly alike. We wouldn't have to speak sometimes – we just knew what the other was thinking.' No wonder he was moved to write about Brookes in this song.

Fame and riches had not yet settled on Paul. They did not encumber him or tweak his suspicions. He could relax with Brookes, trust him a lot more than he could those such as me, who entered his life later, when he was a national figure. As much as he loved me, I felt there was always a little voice in his head looking at me, asking, 'What's his game? When will he make his move?' Steve Brookes never threatened Paul in such a manner.

The boys' relationship was further strengthened when Steve ran into parental problems that raised the possibility of him having to leave Woking. 'Fuck that,' Paul said instantly when Brookes told him, 'you can come and live with us.' Which Brookes did – a great example of John and Ann's generosity towards their son and others. The Wellers of Woking were not the richest in town.

Paul and Steve did everything important together. They drank beer, smoked dope, spent summers at Woking's outdoor swimming pool smoking endless cigarettes and eyeing up the bikinis that waltzed in front of them, and of course they formed a band which Paul's sister, Nicola, named The Jam. The first drummer was Neil Harris; he was replaced by Paul Buckler. Steve thinks Paul hated having two Pauls in the band, hence the name Rick being bestowed upon the sticksman. Dave Waller (see A Man Of Great Promise) played rhythm guitar, but his interests lay elsewhere. Bruce Foxton was brought in to play bass, Paul taking over Waller's position. Brookes remained on lead guitar. They worried about Bruce's David Cassidy-style haircut, but when he sang the Beatles song This Boy at his audition, they were convinced. The band, however, belonged to Steve and Paul. The aim, the idea, hatched during intense tee conversations, was for the band to produce highly commercial and successful pop singles, and then expand musically on the album tracks. Just like a group starting with B . . .

They recorded demos, many of which can now be found on the bootleg circuit. Weller's dad, John, (see Call Me) hawked them around. No one was interested. Then, in 1975, fate struck, because that's when Paul went to see Dr Feelgood at the nearby Guildford Civic Hall. Much has been made of the impact on Paul when he saw The Pistols at the Lyceum, but I think this gig is far more important in the development of The Jam.

The Feelgoods played intense, sharp shocks of r'n'b. Their band had two visual points: the menacing stare and harmonica playing of Lee Brilleaux, and the unique guitar style of Wilko Johnson, who would move constantly across the stage, chopping out great lines of r'n'b riffs, always dressed in a black suit and topped off by a weird haircut. Wilko Johnson was a one-off, and Paul fell for him instantly. 'For anyone who hadn't seen Wilko's stage persona,' Steve Brookes writes, 'it was like a mod killer zombie on crack. I rated the Feelgoods, but Wilko really had a big effect on Paul – the clothes, the hair, the way he moved. It wasn't long ~ this that Paul discovered The Who, and he finally he direction he'd been seeking. The mod thing much to me, and the new direction in ed to take The Jam conflicted with the lanned . . .' quickly assimilated the Wilko style, as evidenced by a 1976 demo of a song entitled Again, where Paul welds one of Wilko's famous guitar patterns on to the Bob Dylan vocal line from Subterranean Homesick Blues, even making a reference to opening up a window to see which way the wind blows. This shift in direction was not to Brookes' liking. When Paul suggested they all troop off to Burton's clothes shop and kit themselves out in black suits *à la* Wilko, Brookes knew the end was near. 'There was no way I was going to be a Wilko look-alike, but as it was three against one I didn't have much choice. It was big decision time. John [Weller] seemed to be the most disappointed when I announced my resignation.'

Steve played out a handful of gigs and then left Woking altogether, heading off to north London. Months later, he got an unexpected phone call. It was Paul, calling from a phone box. The house phone had been cut off, as normal. Paul told him that EMI had been showing some interest in the band; would he consider rejoining? 'Paul always had quite a shy, almost nervous telephone manner for someone so outspoken, and on this occasion probably even more so,' wrote Brookes. At first, Brookes felt excited; then further thought allowed 'all the doubts to come crashing in'. He turned Paul down – a decision that would have rubbed Paul up the wrong way, that's for sure. He had extended a conciliatory hand, which he did not do very often, and had it spurned. Naturally, the boys drifted further apart.

They met up again in 1977. John and

see Steve play a solo show, then invited him over to their new house on the Maybury estate. Steve made the trip a couple of weeks later. 'Paul and I had plenty of time to put aside all our differences and it was a genuine pleasure to see one another again,' he writes. After playing him some of the songs from the *Modern World* album, Paul took Steve to the pub, where they got drunk, stood in the toilet and professed brotherly love for each other. They hugged, and kissed in the way friends do. Then an old man walked into the toilet. 'Oh gawd fuck me,' he exclaimed. Paul and Steve's immediate response was to link arms and mince out of the toilet, 'like a couple of hairdressers'.

Later on, when The Jam were nationally established, Steve set up a guitar shop in Brookwood, a small village near Woking. The band came down and opened the place for him. They drank most of the beer while they were there.

In 1981, Steve took a phone call from John. The band were playing a charity gig at the Woking YMCA; could he supply the equipment? Steve agreed to the request, even though that day he was flying back from N York. When he arrived jet-lagged at the gig, he   on various grumbles about the standard of   . Worse, after the gig the band left with-   ve, even though they had arranged to   d a meal with their former band   pub,' he writes, 'and couldn't   ater that year, Brookes   rd Civic Hall. Again, he sensed a 'frosty reception' and left pretty quickly.

With the guitar shop now failing, Brookes decided to sell up and take a long break travelling round the States. The night before his departure he went out for drinks with friends and ended up in an Indian restaurant where Paul and his then girlfriend Gill and some friends were also eating. Paul was drunk. Steve went over to say hello to him. 'I wished I hadn't,' he writes. 'As my planned trip across America was a first for me, I was quite excited about it, but Paul reacted by sending me up, which didn't really amuse me. In fact I felt pretty humiliated and went back to my table thinking, what an arsehole he's turned into.' That famous sharp tongue (see Porcelain Gods) had once again unleashed itself. Steve and Paul didn't speak for years.

In 1992 I interviewed Steve for a documentary on Paul entitled *Highlights and Hangups*. Two years later I invited him to a surprise birthday party for Paul, held on the day he received an Ivor Novello award. The party was at the Lamb and Flag pub on James Street. (In Style Council days, we often frequented the creperie – or the craperie, as Paul liked to call it – on the corner of St James's Place. The Lamb and Flag is just opposite, so many parties were held there, including a birthday party of mine for which Paul and a few others clubbed together and got me a cappuccino-making machine.) From that night onwards, Paul and Steve began to see each other a lot more. Steve would regularly come to shows. He also came to various parties such as Paul's New Year's Eve party at his house in Ripley in 1999.

At eighteen years of age, Paul shivered at the fragility of relationships, yet he had to locate the truth of their nature. In I Got By In Time, he surmises that bonds can be broken at any time, so the only things you are truly left with are yourself and the one thing that cannot break and cannot be taken away from you, the memories. Those are the things that will keep you going. However bad the break-up, don't worry, in time you will get by, if you have self reliance and a shot of defiance.

FOUR

The Modern World
(*The Modern World*, 1977)

Paul in the Press, and at School

And when he was bad, he was very very bad . . . This
single unashamedly lifts the riff from The Who's song
Pictures Of Lily, and does nothing with it. The song is
musically energetic but not at all compelling, its lyrics
highly defensive, a strange mix of the revelatory and the
trite. It signalled the fact that artistically, Weller had
stalled, a position made clearer by his agreeing to re-
record the song for a single, swapping the word 'fuck'
for 'damn' – an action that speaks volumes.

However, by the time of this song's release in late 1977,
Paul Weller should have been relatively happy. He had
seen his debut album and first two singles chart, he had
sold out Hammersmith Odeon, his band was nationally
established, and he had enjoyed pretty positive press
reviews. That said, the impact saleswise of The Jam was

not great. Their debut album entered the charts at 23, tying with the soundtrack album of *The Black and White Minstrel Show*. The Eagles and Abba held the top spot. (In fact, the latter band would dog Paul for his next four Jam albums, outselling him heavily each time and refusing him entry to the number one spot. No need to elucidate, then, on his thoughts on the pop phenomenon from Sweden.)

The press was important to Paul, the *NME* in particular. In the early seventies, under the guidance of Nick Logan, the *NME* had transformed itself into a unique, indispensable organ, the country's leading music paper, no less. Led by key writers such as Charles Shaar Murray and Nick Kent, and later on Tony Parsons and Julie Burchill, the *NME* was irreverent, important, unmissable. Such was the quality of its writing, it crossed all class barriers. No matter your background, if you were seriously into music, the *NME* was a key element in that experience (see Start!).

Paul not only read the *NME* avidly each week, he also cut out and kept articles significant to him, such as Nick Kent's exemplary Syd Barrett piece, with a Pennie Smith pic of David Bowie on the cover. When he left for his first tour of America in 1977, Paul left strict instructions that his press office at Polydor save every copy of the *NME* for him until he returned. At *NME*, Steve Clarke and Phil McNeil, in particular, supported The Jam. However, a public declaration of support still didn't cut much mustard with Weller. When McNeil travelled to America to interview the band, he walked into the dressing room with a shorter haircut than usual. Paul took one look and activated his defence mechanism by going straight into attack. 'New haircut?' he sneered. 'Office policy, is it, then?'

Over at *Melody Maker*, Chris Brazier filed enthusiastic reports, while at *Record Mirror*, Barry Cain was the main Jam man. At *Sounds*, Chas De Whalley was Paul's greatest supporter. He might have been secretly pleased to make the cover of the *NME* with his very first interview, and with the much-admired Pennie Smith photographing the band, but Paul was not about to bow publicly to anyone. If anything, he deliberately took the opposite road. 'I don't know why you didn't think we were ready to make an album,' he chided De Whalley, who had reviewed *The Modern World* and filed the most positive piece about that poor album, 'cos we're easily the best band around at the moment.' His early interviews are filled with such defensive, arrogant quotes. Here he is later on in the same interview on his contemporaries: 'Instead of just writing songs,' he states, 'people should be writing three-minute classics. That's how I write every song, right? As far as I am concerned, if it's one of mine, it's a classic.' It is instructive, however, to note De Whalley's observation that a lot of Weller's arrogance is actually sheer bravado. For example, Weller tells him, 'If you don't believe you're the best, you never get anywhere.' Whalley then observes, 'Weller's arrogant tone cracks for a moment, and he flashes a knowing smile.'

A knowing smile. Having been a working musician

since the age of fourteen, Weller was wise beyond his years. Already, he knew how the game worked. Just as the working class dress up to present the best picture they can to the world, so Weller presented a strong, determined individual, full of contagious conviction, to his world. Paul knew more than most that The Jam were not firing on all cylinders and that the future was closing in on them. Yet he also knew it was of paramount importance not to admit weakness. Even when all is falling around you, stand tall.

The trouble for Paul was that he couldn't control what the press wrote; nor could he do without them. The *NME* in 1977 was an extremely powerful force. It was commonly referred to as 'the bible'. Any strongly laudatory review, such as Charles Shaar Murray on Patti Smith's debut album, or indeed the piece he wrote on The Jam's third album *All Mod Cons*, could and would shift a significant amount of copies. Paul might have shouted out that he didn't care about reviews, yet barely a year later, prior to the release of *All Mod Cons*, he visited the *NME*'s offices to preview the work to some of the paper's main writers. It was a smart move. The paper was flattered to have such a distinguished visitor, and in return The Jam got some positive pre-album publicity. On the album's release, Murray finished his praise-filled page review with the line, 'Right now, The Jam are the ones to beat.'

And they were. Not long after that, the *NME* annual poll became the preserve of The Jam. Best Band, Best Songwriter, Best Single, Best Album, all went to the

Woking trio, year after year after year. In this manner, the *NME* made The Jam their band. Many writers there, such as Tony Parsons, Paul Du Noyer, Tony Stewart and Neil Spencer, held Paul in great regard.

Paul had respect for a few of these *NME* writers, but in general he was pretty contemptuous of the rock-writing fraternity. Early on, he detected an arrogance in many which infuriated him – though the reason for his dislike of the process of being interviewed could be a lot more frivolous than that. Nick Kent interviewed Paul at the time of The Jam's fourth album, *Setting Sons*. Halfway through the interview, Paul pulled out. Later, I asked him why. 'Well, we had lunch,' he replied, 'and it is pretty hard [making a reference to Mr Kent's some-what hazy condition on that day] to pour your heart out to someone who has half a lettuce leaf on their cheek.'

In 1981, Paul suggested to the *NME* that instead of an interview he write an article about rock writers. The paper agreed to the idea, but when the finished piece arrived they refused to publish. Instead, *Jamming* magazine, a popular fanzine run by devoted Jam fan Tony Fletcher, printed the article. This is what Weller had to say about the music press (the phrase 'blunt speaking' kind of springs to mind . . .): 'Some of the writers are very nice people – quite *real* and honest – but I would say the majority are wankers, a lot worse than the pop stars they write about, and that's saying some-thing. Some I have met really believe they are something special, that you, dear reader, rely on them totally to give you the info and views that you desperately need –

This is true! They honestly believe they are up there with the Big Cogs of the Wheels of Music. Fucking hilarious, innit?' The phrase pot calling the kettle black springs to mind.

Paul was far more relaxed, far more expansive when it came to fanzine interviews. These were conducted by fresh-faced kids of his own age, and for them he opened up far more than he did with the established journalists. He cracked jokes, casually slagged off other bands, and stated his views, of which he was always more than certain.

Ironic, then, that one of the real sour notes presswise came via the fanzine system. A comment in the gossip column of the premier punk fanzine *Sniffing Glue* so enraged Paul that he set fire to the offending copy on stage at the Roxy one night. This is what the anonymous writer wrote: 'We interviewed The Jam the other day but they blew it. All they did was lark about, that's why we've not printed it. They played the new Roxy Club the other day and they were so laid back I thought it was a demotape gone wrong. As [*Glue* writer] Steve Mick says, "The Jam are tight but so are Led Zeppelin. The Jam are 'doing something' but so are Led Zeppelin. Yeah, The Jam should really sort themselves out . . ."' It would have been the phrase 'laid back' that infuriated Paul, just as it does today.

Paul agreed to an interview with the fanzine and strongly defended himself. Again, his conservative nature came to the fore as he explained the band's musical technique, its tightness. When asked what his ambitions were, Paul replied, 'To get somewhere so I can . . . so people can recognize me and respect me . . .' He also displayed his knowledge of pop history, defending the hippy movement and praising them for their 'positive' contributions – this at a time when the word 'hippy' was akin to using a racist term today. Was it *Sniffing Glue*, then, that elicited The Modern World's famous line about Paul not giving 'two fucks about your review'? Probably.

Of course, there were many in the mainstream press who were not at all impressed by Paul's talent. For them, Paul was, and always will be, a dull boy, his music horrifically conservative, an affront to rock's principles of rebellion and sonic expansion. In later years, Everett True at *Melody Maker* would regularly review Paul's records with just one word: wanker. (Paul always asked me to point Everett out to him if we were ever in the same public space. Thankfully, for Everett, that occasion never arose.) Chris Roberts, Simon Reynolds and many others simply couldn't understand the fuss. Nor could ex-*NME* writer Paul Morley, who once stated on TV that for him, Paul was as glamorous as a 'council office worker'. Allan Jones at *Melody Maker* thought him 'a musical hod carrier'. It is interesting how their insults were all based on traditional working-class jobs, giving some credibility to Paul's analysis of the matter. 'Class warfare,' he would simply state whenever we spoke about a particularly vicious review. 'Telling you, mate, it is class warfare. They hate me because I'm not one of them.'

Paul always despised the 'swots', the meek wimps he encountered at school who conformed to authority, who were unable to make their way in the world of physical work. Paul was not against education, far from it, but he despised this breed for they contained no lust for the earthier things in life. 'Not having a go against your lot,' he would often say to me, 'but they can't fucking drink, can they? And the clothes they wear . . .' To receive criticism from such people was a personal affront to Paul.

'For about a day and a half,' he told *Smash Hits* in 1981, 'you might walk round in a daze because someone has said something very personal about you. But if you believe what you are doing is right . . .' Ultimately, The Jam was such a popular band that papers knew that to attack them consistently would be a foolish move on their behalf.

With his next band, The Style Council, Weller still commanded great press interest, although reviews and interviews certainly took on a more confrontational nature. The ending of The Jam and the very singular nature of the Council mystified, indeed angered, many. Writers such as X. Moore at *NME* could never fathom why Weller had swopped agit-prop rock for agit-prop soul, jazz, Latin, etc. Weller still had many supporters, but now a more antagonistic tone began to appear in interviews and reviews. Since 1978 he had regularly been asked, how has fame affected you? Now all anybody wanted to know was, why did you break up The Jam?

At the same time, tabloids such as the *Sun* and the *Daily Mirror* began to take a great interest in pop and its stars, placing the likes of Boy George and Duran Duran on their front pages to attract the youth coin. In agreeing to such coverage, these bands set themselves up, the tabloids often attacking them with vicious forays into their lives and personal habits, usually when sales had started to slump. For reasons such as these, Weller has consistently refused tabloid coverage. Papers such as the *Sun*, with its garish headlines and leering stance, represented to Paul a crass dumbing down within popular culture. Their rabid support of Margaret Thatcher in the 1980s won them no favour with Weller. 'The tabloids cut your fucking bollocks off,' he stated, with typical élan, in 2002. 'You cease to be seen as an artist, a songwriter, and you just become a face in the paper. It's dangerous.' As a consequence, Weller has remained a significant absentee from today's brash celebrity culture – a decision that has won him much respect from his audience.

When the Council ran out of steam, Weller began the arduous process of putting together his solo career. It took him four years of blood, sweat and tears to regain his position and audience, a fact acknowledged in 1993 when the *NME* placed him on its cover, the first time he had appeared on it since 1986.

The arrival of magazines such as *Mojo* and *Uncut*, with their emphasis on classic music, provided a great forum for Paul. He was regularly interviewed by them and always agreed to submitting lists of songs he was listening to, or speaking about acts he adored. He was a presence in the broadsheets as well. Their arts pages and magazines regularly delivered intelligent but very safe features which all tended to follow the same path: he was in The Jam, he still makes good music, he has five kids, he doesn't like politicians any more, he lives a normal life, good on him.

Paul, though, remained guarded in such encounters, meeting journos in restaurants and cafés, offering up enough to fill the pages but nothing more. It's a game he knows backwards. 'When you have an album coming out,' he said in May 2000, 'you do some press, some radio and TV, then tour. It doesn't make my heart sink, but you know what it's going to be like.' It is only when he gets drunk that his famously sharp tongue comes to the fore, and the article carries a bit more bite.

And do not think that positive press always meets with his approval. I recall one Sunday morning handing him a copy of the *Observer* which carried a quite complimentary review of one of his shows. I thought he would like the piece. I should have known better with a boy like him. He read about three paragraphs and then, without warning, viciously chucked the rag away. 'Fucking silly writers,' he shouted, with real venom. 'They always get it fucking wrong.' I went to the kitchen, got out of the way, made coffee.

Did Paul anticipate this level of interest in him from day one? Certainly, in this Modern World song, the twenty-year-old songwriter states unequivocally that he is on his way to the top, he has known his destiny from an early age, and no one but no one is going to stop him. OK? His arrogance and determination are there to hear, and easy to dismiss. But every word is true. Weller knew at fourteen that he was going to be a musician. With that decision came the certainty of success. He then put all his energies into realizing his destiny.

School was the very first thing to be jettisoned. Documentation of these times is flimsy. Weller at school is not a rich field of study, but there are some intriguing items to consider, not least from the man himself. In 1980, he sat down and wrote a piece for *Flexipop* magazine on his time at Sheerwater Secondary School in Woking, a tough school he dreaded attending, such was its reputation for mayhem and violence. 'Sheerwater had a really bad reputation,' he explains. 'There were loads of stories about what the older pupils used to do to the new kids.' Despite this, or probably because of this, Weller kept his head down. 'For the first two years at Sheerwater I really tried to get stuck in, y'know. I really tried to work hard, but I gave up by the third year. I couldn't be fucking bothered.' The cause of his dissent? 'I started discovering sex, music and drinking, and there was no way I was going to stay in and do some poxy maths homework.'

There was another factor involved in Weller's abrupt withdrawal from daily class life. Sheerwater Secondary was not a school of excellence. Its main purpose was to produce a workforce for local factories such as John Walker in Woking or Brown's in Bisley. Most of the children lived on the surrounding council estates. At my school, St John the Baptist, we were always wary of Sheerwater kids – Paul instinctively hated the place and its authoritarian structure. Moreover, to be ignored or patronized by people he despised was more than his fierce pride could take. 'At school,' he writes, 'I hated all my teachers passionately. They were all bastards and bitches, talking to me as if I was nothing. School is where I decided I would show bastards like that that I didn't need their rules or education to get anywhere in life.'

In that respect, Sheerwater was the perfect school for Paul. It inadvertently created the inspiration, the drive he talks about in this song. 'I suppose I do have some happy memories of school life,' he continues, 'but most of my school recollections are very painful. I don't like other people having authority over me and that's why I hated the teachers. I was 14 when I started to learn to play the guitar and it was at the same age I decided that was what I was gonna do in life. That decision gave me so much inner strength. Once I had decided, I completely switched off at school. I just didn't bother any more. I knew it was all a waste of fucking time.'

There was only one subject Paul excelled at: poetry. He was good at technical drawing as well, but it was in the field of language that he best expressed himself. It was also at Sheerwater that he first encountered an English writer who would have a huge effect on his art: George Orwell. Paul read Orwell's classic book *1984* for the first time at Sheerwater, and the school allowed him to enter a poem, 'Room 101', based on the book, for his

CSE. It was one of their very few concessions to their most reluctant pupil. Paul Weller left school as soon as he could, and he never once looked back.

Instead, he got to do something no one else at his school did: he grew up in public.

FIVE

Tonight At Noon
(*The Modern World*, 1977)

Other People's Music

Every art form has a different take on the subject of plagiarism. Cinema, for example. In his film *The Untouchables*, director Brian De Palma recreates the iconic steps scene from Eisenstein's famous 1925 film *Battleship Potemkin*. But De Palma is not blatantly stealing, he is 'paying homage'. In painting and in conceptual art, the same principle applies: the artist is not stealing, he is paying a tribute. In literature, it's slightly different: if a writer should appropriate the style of another, then he is 'cleverly parodying' that writer.

In music, however, there is no get-out clause. Lift a riff, a melody, a chorus line, a middle eight, a sound, the lyrics, then you are a charlatan, a thief, sir, and you should be publicly chastised.

This aberration may stem from the way pop

developed during the late fifties and sixties. Bands tended to inspire one another in those flowering days, pushed one another to higher musical delights. Someone used a sitar, another would reply by using a classical orchestra. Today, someone uses a sitar, ten others do as well. The result was that as pop grew up it became incumbent on artists to be 'fresh', 'original' and 'individual'. Bob Dylan certainly passed that test, while those who copied him (Donovan, Barry McGuire) were vilified as thieves. The fact that Dylan himself was liberally borrowing from a variety of sources was either swept under the carpet or not spotted by those so dazzled by his mercurial sound, incredible use of language and intriguing persona.

During his solo career, Paul settled on the Royal Albert Hall as his main London venue. He liked performing at this elegant hall, and would often play a run of two or three concerts there. When the run ended, Paul would always celebrate, maybe ending up in a West End club, drinking till dawn. What intrigued me was that without fail, at some point in the night he would turn to me and say, 'Got away with it again,' and raise his glass, as though he had just pulled off a major bank robbery. I was slightly puzzled by this attitude. I knew Paul lifted from other people, but so does every other musician. That's why Paul was always delighted when he heard a record which someone else had ripped off. Perhaps I just hadn't appreciated the scope of his magpie tendencies. This song, for example.

Tonight At Noon is the stand-out track from the

Modern World album. The title comes from a Charlie Mingus album which the Liverpool poet Adrian Henri also appropriated for one of his poems. Paul liked Henri, and the work of his fellow Liverpudlian poets Roger McGough and Brian Patten. They sought to bring poetry down from its lofty position, and relocate it on the streets. Their poems contained recognizable, everyday objects, yet their themes were timeless, thus creating a kind of durable pop art poetry. These three poets were famously published together in a book called *The Mersey Sound* – a nod towards their city's great musical heritage.

In that book, Henri published the aforementioned Tonight At Noon as well as In The Midnight Hour, a love poem that talks about nightflowers, dripping trees, walking down muddy lanes, walking in city squares in winter rain, the country girl . . . In Tonight At Noon, the first acoustic song The Jam released, Paul sings about nightflowers, dripping trees, walking down muddy lanes, walking in city squares in winter rain, the country girl. Although on the album's back cover Paul thanks Henri for 'foresight and inspiration', Henri does not appear on the writing credits, despite Paul lifting several lines from his poem wholesale. He also took the title of another Henri poem, 'I want to paint', and wrote a song about it which remains unreleased to this day. Nor do Lennon and McCartney get a nod either. After all, it was their song Ticket To Ride that gave Paul his opening riff. Yet, despite all this, Weller proves his point by creating a lovely song which, musically at least, rises above plagiarism to stand as one of Paul's best compositions during this uneasy period in his creative life.

Given the workload Paul set himself – an album a year, one-off singles, quality B sides – it is no wonder that accusations of plagiarism have dogged him throughout his career. Indeed, on his very own website fans seem to take great delight in tracking down the man's sources. Here's what 'The Woodcutter's Son' had to say:

> Weller stole so much. The hook for In The City he stole from The Who's song, also called In The City; he nicked loads of riffs off The Kinks; Standards pretty much comes from Can't Explain, while Modern World is borrowed from Pictures of Lily; The Gift is a carbon copy of some old Small Faces song (forget which one right now) [it was Don't Burst My Bubble]. Precious is Pig Bag; Town Called Malice is Martha Reeves and the Vandellas; Sunflower's opening riff is taken right from a Fleur de Lys song; Out in the Universe is from Thunderclap Newman . . . and so on. That said, no complaints. He's a master at taking old riffs and tweaking them into something new, unlike Noel Gallagher who – after the 1st LP, anyway – was too $%£!"*(lazy to even do that much!!

'The guitar intro to The Bitterest Pill is the theme tune to *Bagpuss*,' points out '2daysYoungMod', while 'No 5' thinks that the guitar solo from The Gift is lifted from the instrumental bit in Watcha Gonna Do About

It (Small Faces). The Style Council song Me Ship Came In nicked the chords from Song For My Father by Horace Silver, and the solo Weller anthem Changing Man has the same descending chord structure as The Beatles' Dear Prudence.

A different perspective on this subject came from a Chris Ferguson:

> Look at any artist with an extensive back catalogue and you will find lots of coincidences and possible rip-offs. Similar styles of music are littered with examples – loads of old soul stuff is basically reworkings of hits of the time, but I don't think Weller has really done it with any kind of cunning intent to con anyone.
>
> I think the Taxman/Start thing could almost be seen in the same light as the way many dance and rap songs sample extensively – he took a riff and wrote his own song around it and it works. I don't see any problem with doing that personally.
>
> I'd prefer that any day of the week to a band or singer who pointlessly imitates his idols and ends up devoid of any original thoughts. You probably know who I mean without me upsetting their fans . . .

SIX

All Mod Cons (*All Mod Cons*, 1978)

Paul and the Business

By 1978, Paul had seen enough of the music business to know its true nature. After the poor reception and sales of the *Modern World* album, he would have instantly noted the cooling off from his record company. Suddenly he was no longer the receiver of smiles and promises. Suddenly he was no longer the golden boy. Only chart positions and record sales counted in this world, nothing else.

Weller memorably made his feelings known on this short sharp shock of an opening track. Addressing a nameless but typical record company lackey, he tells him (or her) the score, that as long as his talent is making them rich, they love him, but if he were to fall, he won't see them for dust.

Weller's attitude drips with bitter irony, his strict

viewpoint one of tough opposition to anything establishment, be that politicians or the music business. This was the Paul of The Jam, a seriously angry, seriously cynical twenty-year-old whose sullen stance had been nurtured in a tough school and a tough town, and then given a purpose by punk. Although The Jam were the 'black sheep' of that movement, Paul passionately believed in certain ideals which punk had inspired in him. In 1981, he said, 'It was punk that changed my ideas a lot. Well, totally. I realised music was more important.' Punk dictated that music had to be exciting, relevant. The audience had to be treated with respect. Paul set out to fulfil these ideals. The Jam became well known for the access they granted their fans, letting them into soundchecks and dressing rooms after gigs. 'I think that's why The Jam clicked,' Paul said in 1995. 'We made our own scene. What we and our audiences were was more to the real spirit of punk.'

Major record companies were quickly cast as one of punk's greatest enemies, and an emphasis was placed on the integrity of independent record labels – a notion that exists to this day. Paul was not particularly interested in small record companies – he wanted his music made public to as big an audience as possible – but that didn't stop him despising the music business. This is him just a year ago talking about going to Universal, the record company that controls his back catalogue: 'I went into Universal to do some press for some Jam reissue the other day and it was like walking into some fucking Wall Street bank. This big fucking place with some cunt sitting behind a desk...' As you can imagine, this statement did not go down too well with the department that handles Paul's back catalogue, most of whom are huge Weller fans.

Weller always expressed to me his hatred of the dichotomy between music and commerce, how music, his precious, sacred music, suddenly became a commodity in the hands of a record company. 'They might as well be selling fucking baked beans,' he often remarked. Within the business he did come across people who actually liked music – Eugene Manzi at London Records, for example, whom he subsequently befriended – but in the main he viewed all music business employees with huge disdain. I recall how disgusted he was at the time of his involvement in the political movement Red Wedge when a record company head told singer Junior Giscombe not to get involved 'as it might hurt his career'.

Weller, like most musicians, disliked record companies, feeling that they were duplicitous and, given the slightest opportunity, would rob you blind. He always said that artists did not receive proper royalty rates. 'They have this clause in the contracts,' he told me once, 'where money I earn goes on marketing. Well, how can you work out how much they have spent? It's just another way of them taking my money.' I told him about Keith Richards' remark that he would rather work with the Mafia because 'at least you know they are going to rob you'. Weller enthusiastically agreed with the man.

The company he did offer at least limited praise for was Andy MacDonald's Independiente label, for whom Weller made five solo albums. 'You walk in and the MD is smoking a spliff and playing the guitar,' he once said. 'That's my kind of company.'

Weller's most famous run-in with the music business happened in 1988 when he got himself into a serious altercation with David Munns, the head of his company. Munns, a bluntly spoken man, had recently taken over Polydor Records at a time when Weller's record sales with The Style Council had dipped dramatically. Despite this downturn in fortunes, the company was, according to former Polydor employee Dennis Munday, contractually obliged to pay the Weller camp a million pounds an album. When Weller delivered the highly experimental album *Confessions Of A Pop Group* and then lobbied for the cover not to carry a picture of himself, tension between band and record company rose dramatically. Munns didn't take Paul up on his offer of fisticuffs, but he did refuse to release the next Style Council album, *A Decade Of Modernism*, thus bringing to a close Paul's first record contract. Paul remained unrepentant about his antagonistic stance towards Munns. 'I'm not used to people talking to me like that,' he haughtily declared when asked about the incident years later. 'I'm from Woking and I don't give a fuck.'

What's ironic is that Paul himself could have ended up in a Munns-style position. After the demise of The Jam, he began a label entitled Respond. It was important to him to use his position positively and creatively. Thanks to his work in The Jam, money was not a huge problem for him, and he was now able to make his base at the Solid Bond Recording Studios at the top of Bayswater Road in London. Respond, he declared, would be a young label. In all his interviews from this period he talks about how vital it is for young bands to come through. Vital, vital, vital.

He signed two young acts, the singer Tracie and a Scottish funk soul band called The Questions, as well as releasing singles by his friend Vaughn Toulouse and a band called A Craze. Tracie had sung on The Jam's final single, Beat Surrender, and the debut single from The Style Council, Speak Like A Child. Paul liked her attitude, her chutzpah, although she would later say that she felt Paul's all-encompassing involvement in the making of her records was not for the best. Still, she had a bright start. On Respond, she scored two top thirty singles, House That Jack Built and Give It Some Emotion. Her debut album, however, stiffed. The Questions didn't even get near the top thirty.

I recall how amazed he used to be by my often lukewarm response after he had played me a Respond record. 'God,' he would say, 'I thought you would be bowled over by that.' I wasn't bowled over for various reasons, such as the bland nature of the songs and the muddy productions. John Weller, who was Paul's manager for many years, wasn't that knocked out by Paul's foray into the music business either. Respond, despite a distribution deal with A&M Records, didn't take off. John didn't like that. Paul saw the bank books and knew that his vision of producing high-quality soul pop records would not be realized. Respond folded quietly, and Paul went back to what he did best, writing songs in an industry he despises to this day.

SEVEN

To Be Someone (Didn't We Have A Nice Time) (*All Mod Cons*, 1978)

Paul and Fame (Part One)

This was Paul's first song about fame, about its pitfalls and what it can do to those seduced by it. Subsequent songs (see Porcelain Gods) adopted a far more personal stance; this tune was more of a manifesto, a curt reminder of the dangers that success brings, and a bitter attack on rock stars in general, to boot.

In a 1978 interview, Weller said that this song's genesis occurred in a van when he was 'thinking about someone who had to pack it all in'. As he did with many of his songs during this period, Paul takes the Ray Davies approach (see Mr Clean) and makes his points through a mix of irony, anger and insight (although the greatest irony of all is that the things he railed against in 1978 he would one day do himself. He would get high with trendy friends, and own a swimming pool. But by then he was a completely different person). The song venomously attacks seventies rock star existence – the pliant reporters, the guitar-shaped swimming pool, the white powders, the girls, the money. For Paul, this lifestyle was an affront, not only because its excesses prevented meaningful music from being made (hence the need for punk), but because it was such a cliché. Paul hated the obvious, or the easy way. With The Jam he sought to create a new kind of 'star', one that remained down to earth, accessible.

Fame did not suit Paul and, according to him, it still doesn't. His shyness and insecurity have compelled him to avoid the spotlight wherever possible. He has always resolutely refused to lead a 'celebrity' life; he is simply not cut out for it. Showbiz parties and trendy night-clubs hold no interest for him. 'I hate being famous,' he recently said. 'It's fucking rubbish . . . There's nothing you can do about being famous, it's out of your control. I'm just here to make records and make music.' The reality is, Paul not only likes a certain kind of fame – people approaching and complimenting him gracefully – he *needs* fame as a way of validating his work and maintaining his world within a world.

Yet the act of seeking fame throws up a major contradiction. Here is someone whose teenage character is painfully shy, shot through with enough insecurities to keep psychiatrists in employment for years to come, yet he is spending his time dreaming of, and actively seeking, attention. 'Creative people,'

Anthony Storr observes in *The Dynamics of Creation*, 'possess an unusual combination of qualities, rather than one particular attribute. It is the tension between those two opposites, and the need to resolve this tension, which provides the motive force for creation.' He later adds that a schizoid personality is often detected in creative people, and that 'since most creative activity is solitary, choosing such an occupation means that the schizoid person can avoid the problems of direct relationships with others. If he writes, paints or composes, he is of course communicating. But it is a communication entirely on his own terms. The whole situation is within his control.'

Paul is a control freak – a man who used his talent to build his own universe. Yet this environment needs success for it to function properly – success is its oxygen. That is why Paul not only likes but needs a certain amount of fame. The tension, then, is between Paul's competitive, ambitious nature and his urgent need to retreat from a world he finds too unstable, filled with humans he fundamentally distrusts. Paul hid himself from the outset, trusted very few people. In later years, however, as his confidence in himself soared and his ego was awoken by accolades from the next generation of bands, his social circle widened considerably. Therefore, the effect of thirty years of fame on Paul Weller has been varied.

For the Paul Weller of The Jam, fame was initially a buzz. 'I liked it at first,' he admitted in 1995, 'because that was part of the fantasy when I was a kid, to be whatever The Beatles were.' It quickly became a drag, though, as the fame Paul experienced was of the obsessive kind. For thousands of people, Paul Weller was an absolute hero, not only for his ability to write tough, memorable songs which poetically reflected British working-class life, but also for his un-compromising attitude. Even today, he elicits a powerful response from old Jam fans. The other day I had my house valued. The guy who came was in his mid-forties, quiet, professional. He went about his business until he saw a picture on the hallway wall of Paul and me together.

'You've met Paul Weller?' he suddenly exclaimed. 'That was my band, the fucking Jam, that was my group!'

Yours and a million others, friend. 'Paul Weller,' the Creation Records owner Alan McGee recently wrote, 'was the most important man in popular culture because we all felt he was one of us.'

Such was the devotion Weller inspired in his audience, a consistent question during his Jam days was, 'Do you think fame has changed you?' It was asked because fame of such magnitude should make a difference, but no one could detect any overt change in this man who acted so normally. 'I don't know how success affects me,' he once mused. 'I don't think it affects me in an egotistical way. Whenever I say that people think I am being complacent. But I am not. I find fame unnerving, embarrassing.' In 1982, he said, 'I can't feel special because I am Paul Weller and The Jam had number one hits. I can feel special because

I am me, so anyone can potentially feel this way.'

For that vast audience of his, Paul Weller was a magician. His ability to crystallize in three verses all aspects of their lives, then wrap it up in contagious, sharp, melodic music, gave him a status that was beyond normal pop hysteria. No band in recent times has represented the young men of the working class with such skill and passion and vigour. His refusal to change or play the game, his determination to remain the same despite the pressures, was widely applauded. It was why every Jam single and album was eagerly awaited. What was Paul going to bring down from the mountain this time?

At that time, Weller saw his music as a force to change people, to change society, to make lives better, to inspire people to better things. Pop stardom wasn't the goal. Nor was the fans' mad devotion to him. 'I used to be on stage singing all these songs about being an individual,' he told me once, 'and all I could see in front of me was just a sea of green parkas.'

He could not escape this hysteria. He told me once how when living in Pimlico he popped into the local pub to buy some ciggies. Within minutes, a crowd of drunken geezers had got hold of him and were throwing him up in the air, as if it was his birthday. I recall a Sunday afternoon gig we went to near King's Cross in the early eighties and Paul being pinned so tightly against the wall by about fifty kids that I thought he would suffocate. He nearly did at a gig in Newcastle. Paul rushed through a crowd of fans, two of whom simultaneously grabbed either end of his scarf and nearly strangled him.

Paul struggled with fame in his Jam days. In my first *Melody Maker* interview with him, I asked if he felt at all special. In what way? he wanted to know. For escaping Woking, carving out the life he wanted from his teenage dreams. 'Well I do,' he said reluctantly, 'but I hate saying it. It makes me different from everyone else.' During that period, it was of huge importance to Paul that he not be seen placing himself above others. Instead, he liked to quote the Stevie Wonder song Uptight, the line about no one being better than I, and knowing I'm just an average guy.

He once told me that his favourite analysis of fame was made by the philosopher and TV presenter Malcolm Muggeridge. Muggeridge said that fame divided you into two. One day you go out and you get so angry with people bugging you that all you want in the whole wide world is to be left alone so you can go about your business. The next time you go out, your wish is granted. No one talks to you. No one looks at you. But instead of being pleased, now all you're thinking is, have I lost my popularity? Doesn't anyone like me any more? 'That is exactly how I feel,' Paul told me several times. 'It's a right bastard.'

In general, Paul was gracious with his admirers, although he would always be seriously irked by people blatantly staring at him. One time, Paul had Noel Gallagher in his Mini. He stopped at a zebra crossing to allow a young man to walk across. The man looked over and saw not one but two of Britain's most famous faces sat in a car together. He couldn't believe his eyes, stared the whole time it took to cross. 'What you fucking looking at?' Weller finally shouted at him. Paul got the 'stare' a lot. It unnerved him, made him feel uncomfortable, as it would do most people. He wasn't, as he often told me, an animal in a cage.

The solo-career Paul Weller accepts fame with a lot more ease. For some, this proved to be a mistake. His first wife, Dee C. Lee, pointed out in the *Into Tomorrow* documentary that when people used to come up and tell him how great he was, 'it just bounced off him'. Today, she says, he takes these compliments on board and the subtext of that remark is how much this ego driven behaviour has changed him, and not for the better. That said, I never once saw Paul refuse anyone an autograph or a picture. Even when he was in a rush, he would always try to accommodate a request. His favourite kind of people were those who told him how much his music – or, better still, certain songs – meant to them. He liked that kind of praise, for it validated him and his work. 'I was in a shop the other day,' he once remarked, 'and a girl came up and told me how much my song Brand New Start meant to her. Really cool, it was.'

On other occasions, he had to draw the line. On tour in Sheffield one time we were sat at the hotel bar when a newly-wed couple came in. They couldn't believe it. That very morning they had got married to Paul's song Wild Wood. Paul was genuinely touched. He told them

PAOLO HEWITT

he was very honoured. Which he was. But then the couple pushed it further. Their reception was at the hotel that night; would Paul get on stage and play Wild Wood for them? Paul declined. They pushed on with the request. Paul said no. The couple pleaded. Paul declined again, and then, to get rid of them, started talking to someone else at the bar. The couple got the hint, and walked.

It wasn't just ordinary folk who adored him. Many musicians (see Walls Come Tumbling Down) were huge fans. So were actors such as Martin Freeman (a huge Style Council fan), Ray Winstone and, funnily enough, Michael Douglas and Catherine Zeta Jones. The night before a gig in Los Angeles, Paul watched the film *Traffic*, starring those two actors. Next day, at the gig, one of the roadies came into the dressing room and said, 'Michael Douglas and Catherine Zeta Jones are outside, want to know if it's OK to come in.'

Paul thought it was a wind-up. 'How did you know I watched that film last night?' he asked.

'No, Paul, Michael Douglas and . . .'

Eventually, Hollywood's golden couple came in and expressed their very real admiration for his work.

In The Jam and The Style Council, Paul struggled with fame and its consequences. Now he is far more relaxed about it. He no longer fights with his ego, as he once told me he did on a regular basis back in the eighties. Today, he knows his worth, and is unafraid to acknowledge it. The Paul Weller of The Jam would hate the Paul Weller of today.

EIGHT

Mr Clean (*All Mod Cons*, 1978)

Paul, Ray Davies, Class and Character Writing

To write this crucial third album, Paul Weller retreated back to Woking from his Pimlico flat and got down to serious work. The Jam were being written off, attacked from all sides. Demos they had recorded had been dismissed by their A&R man, Chris Parry. Live reviews were scathing. Interest in the band was waning. Paul now dedicated himself to re-establishing The Jam. 'I didn't go out at all', he said in 1980 of that period. 'I just stayed in and wrote.'

Music had always inspired him, and if there was one artist who would prove to be the most vital springboard for Weller at this point, it was Ray Davies, the driving creative force behind The Kinks. It is a love affair that continues to this day. Weller was always talking up Davies to me. I knew a lot about this great songwriter, but Paul's interest went much deeper. He particularly adored those songs where Davies matched his peerless melodies with a unique lyrical angle. I'm thinking of Kinks songs such as Two Sisters, Some Mother's Son, Did You See His Face, and particularly that classic song Days. I remember one night Paul playing that song to me repeatedly, shaking his head in admiration at its power and grace.

Although he dismissed most of the man's work in the 1970s, Davies's declining powers at this point fascinated him. I remember a phone conversation during which Paul told me he had spent some time listening to Kinks albums from the seventies.

'How were they?' I asked.

'Dreadful. I've just thrown them all in the bin. What happens to these people? How can they put out so much crap? They all seem to run out of melody.'

The subtext was clear: was this Paul's fate, to run out of steam?

As it turned out, Paul was highly impressed with Davies's last solo album, *Other People's Lives* (2006). It appeared on Paul's current record label, V2 Records. 'I wasn't meant to have a copy,' Paul told me when we were in Spain in 2005, 'but someone slipped me an early preview copy and told me not to tell anyone I had it, least of all Ray Davies, who would have gone spare. So of course I got off my tits and played the album again and again and again – you know what I get like. So at five in the morning I ring this guy to get Ray's number and tell him what a fucking great album it was, but luckily he didn't answer his phone. Otherwise I would have been on the phone to Ray Davies going, I love you, Ray, I really love you . . .'

Ray Davies had always been an individual. While his sixties contemporaries sang of love and colours, of street fighting men and Indian mystics, Davies made England, its quaint customs, its characters and its unique nature, his obsession. Paul quickly incorporated this idea into his work and began writing about his England, the England of Surrey small-town life, and work and pubs, and the lives contained within.

One of Davies's many techniques was to invent characters which he then lampooned. The dedicated follower of fashion was one, so too was Mr Pleasant. Weller adopts the same technique here, creating the morally bankrupt Mr Clean. Only Weller does not lampoon this man; he threatens him in such a manner that Pete Townshend of The Who once called this 'the most menacing song' he had ever heard.

It certainly reeks of violence. The main riff is latent anger personified, waiting to explode, Weller's lyrics a series of overt threats, promising to 'fuck up' the guy's life and 'stick his face in the grinder'. Weller recently revealed that the song's inspiration was drawn from an incident in a hotel bar. His then girlfriend Gill fell over and a bystander rushed to help her to her feet. As he did so, Weller noted the man's hands discreetly caressing his girlfriend's chest. No wonder this song brims with such anger.

Mr Clean is today a dying breed, a once archetypal middle Englander who catches the train to London from suburbia, reads *The Times*, wears a bowler hat and carries a briefcase, is full of class snobbery and espouses high moral values. All the time, though, he lusts after secretaries, and gets pissed. For Weller ('I have always been class conscious'), this is the true enemy. Don't forget me or my kind, he warns him, because one day . . . Tellingly, there is none of the irony he employs on most of *All Mod Cons*, just hatred, pure hatred, which he knew his audience would latch on to with glee. For this was the sound of class warfare, the reason why Weller would soon be the working boy's absolute hero.

NINE

English Rose (*All Mod Cons*, 1978)

Paul and Englishness

Written on tour in America, written for his girlfriend Gill who he was badly missing, English Rose was famously never credited on *All Mod Cons*, Weller admitting to embarrassment at writing such a touching ballad. Nearly thirty years old now, the song shows no signs of ageing and remains a staple of weddings and those compilation tapes made by lovers still flushed with desire and love.

The song was prompted by Weller's uncomfortable relationship with America at the time, and his youthful yearning for England. At first, he did not like the States, a feeling that strengthened when straight ahead rock audiences threw items of rubbish at him as he and The Jam performed before making way for the tour head-liners, the heavy-metal-tinged band Blue Oyster Cult.

America was vast, and so different to the England Paul knew and loved. Where England was discreet, they were loud; where England was polite, they were rude; where England had formality, America knew no table manners. Paul struggled with America for many years, though eventually he changed his opinion on this vast continent, having come to appreciate that it was not just one soul that governed the American character, but a million different ones.

He still preferred England, though. As he says, 'no matter where I roam, I will return to my English rose,' an obvious metaphor for his country as well as his loved one.

Weller and England are very much bound up with each other. In his character, many differing strains of Englishness compete against one another. Paul can be the perfect English gentleman, the gracious host, Savile Row smart, a ringer for John Steed of *The Avengers* (he once parodied that very character for an *NME* Christmas special in 1982). Yet, just as easily, the virulent side of Englishness can be detected in him, the one you see at football tournaments abroad, the drunken yob exercising and seeking violence, sometimes simply for violence's sake – hence the *Clockwork Orange* fixation. Weller can be romantic poet or revolutionary soldier, thug or gentleman (he would have been perfect for the French Revolution). Other English traits he carries in his soul include great parsimony, stubbornness, conservatism, a love of order, and a desire for good manners.

The culture he springs from, the culture of smart music and smart clothes which has directed the majority of British youth post war (the ones he has named the Soul Stylists), he absolutely treasures. The fact that England gave the world Mod and the sixties, John Stephen and Mary Quant and George Orwell and Joe Orton and The Beatles, The Kinks, The Small Faces, and a million great records, that it gave the world Peter Blake, great tailoring and great footballers, is a source of great pride for him. The landscape of Britain, whether in the cold or heat, also has special meaning for him, but then so do the cracked roofs, the dark alleyways and the rubbish-strewn high streets of British towns.

Of course, his feelings for this country have over the years veered between love and hatred, pride and disgust – disgust at the dockers coming out for Enoch Powell in the 1960s, pride in the stoic spirit of the working class to endure. Early doors, his mother Ann (see Call Me) was a great influence on him. She is Tory, a strong believer in a structure within society, starting from the royal family downwards. You can hear her views in Paul's assertions in the *NME* about voting Conservative, about admiring the royal family, made in 1977. But Weller's use of the Union Jack at this point was always more bound up in his sixties obsession than in promoting nationalism on any scale (see also The Peacock Suit).

By the start of the 1980s there had been a shift in his understanding of England. His big book at the time was

Geoffrey Ashe's *Visions of Camelot*, a spiritual exploration of the Arthurian legend. This was mystical England Weller was now exploring, the idea that when the country fell to its knees, a great leader would arise and deliver England out of turmoil and into a golden era.

At around the same time, Weller formed one of his most unlikely alliances by working on a song called England I Miss You with East End punk band The Cockney Rejects. Given his dislike for crude, one-dimensional art, the relationship raised eyebrows. The Rejects were high in the Oi band movement, an angry offshoot from punk, their gigs often marred by heavy violence. Their music was hardly the most sophisticated, although many found a boisterous charm in their energetic thrashings. Asked about this session once, Paul replied, 'It was a demo they were working on and I think I helped them out with it, maybe the lyrics. [Paul has a great memory, so I love this vague expression 'maybe the lyrics'. Good tactic. When they have you pinned against a wall, feign memory loss.] But it's a lot of crap, so maybe that's why it never came out officially.' Or maybe Paul had inadvertently been taking his patriotism into slightly dangerous waters, and, seeing the turbulence ahead, had quickly retreated to land.

I asked Paul once if he enjoyed being English. 'I don't know,' he replied. 'I've never been German or French.'

Funny fellows, these English, eh?

TEN

In The Crowd (*All Mod Cons*, 1978)

Paul and Technology

A stand-out track from a stand-out album, this is a fine song, underpinned by a striking riff, memorable words and a series of resounding guitar chords that end in a psychedelic workout. Paul's liking of psychedelia was linked to his love of Syd Barrett, the founder of Pink Floyd. Paul loved Barrett's work with the Floyd, and the man's two solo albums. He always held 'dear Syd', as he called him, in much affection.

In the DVD made for the thirtieth anniversary of the release of The Jam's third album *All Mod Cons* (which Paul felt was good but had 'too much of Hewitt and [Gary] Crowley on it'), Paul reveals that it was the Mick Jones song Lost In The Supermarket that inspired this tune. The thirtieth anniversary of *All Mod Cons* actually falls in 2008, and The Clash's album *London Calling*, which contains the song Paul refers to, was released a year and a half after *All Mod Cons*.

This song's lyrical theme is derived in part from Paul's reading of George Orwell's *1984* (see The Modern World) in which the main character, Winston Smith, rebels against the mass conformity imposed on the people. *1984* was a special book for Paul. He loved the idea of the individual taking on the state and triumphantly succeeding by re-establishing his humanity and life force. Humans over machines every time. This song dwells on its themes, the crowd a place of safety where nobody feels or sees anything, where orders are blindly followed. 'I have a sort of love/hate relationship with crowds,' Paul said in 1978. 'In some ways they are nice and the security is nice, but sometimes I find myself walking around in a supermarket, or in Oxford Street, and I just suddenly come out of myself, drifting aimlessly and going nowhere, doing nothing.'

Paul shared Orwell's fears of an encroaching Big Brother state where our every move is filmed or recorded, hence the song's hugely sarcastic line 'technology is the most', concerning its supposed powers. Paul has always been hugely mistrustful of new inventions, which for a Modernist is a contradictory stance. In fact, so deep is this mistrust, I always thought that if Paul had been a caveman he would have been the first to oppose the invention of the wheel. I can hear him now, waving his club in the air, shouting, 'What do you want that for, eh? Why do you think God gave us two legs?' Paul continually challenged the promises made by technology. Did videos really make people's lives better? How were mobile phones going to enhance lives? His paranoia always kicked in when technology loomed into his life. He often suspected darker forces were at work, deploying their weapons to keep us in our place. 'I have really begun texting a lot,' he told an interviewer. 'I never did before, but you start sending them and the next thing you know, they have got you.'

Paul is, as they say, technologically challenged. He could never work out how to operate videos or DVD machines. I used his ignorance to my advantage. For example, if you lent Paul something, like rare footage of a band he adored, it took a bit of time to get it back, Paul always hoping you would forget to ask for it. To circumvent this problem, if Paul asked to borrow a rare video, I'd just tell him I'd love to lend it to him but his machine wasn't compatible. Such a shame.

Most notoriously, I recall his disdainful and cynical attitude when the internet came into our lives. 'People say it's going to change the world,' he sneered at me one night, 'but it's just another con, keep everybody glued to a screen.' 'I will never have one in my house,' the Mod thundered to an interviewer recently, 'it's the Devil's Window.'

Paul never understood that the creation of one outlet didn't automatically mean the cancelling out of another. People still speak to each other. In fact, texting and emails actually draw us closer together – something messenger pigeons never managed. Enabling millions of people to get in contact actually makes the potential for revolution more real, as certain websites have recently proved. Paul was having none of it.

Once, after a Royal Albert Hall show of Paul's, we ended up back in his garden, drinking and whatever until seven in the morning, the pair of us clutching half-filled glasses in the pale sunlight until Jessie, his daughter, appeared asking for breakfast, and put us back in the real world.

'Do you write on a computer?' he asked me.

'Of course I do,' I replied. 'It's made my life so much easier. I love it.'

'For fuck's sake, don't use one,' he said. 'I hate to think of you writing on one of those fucking things. Go back to a typewriter. I want to hear the click click of a typewriter coming out of your window.'

Where did this hatred arise from? Was it that technological advances were busy creating a society that simply wasn't in his vision? Maybe, but I would say it was more to do with Paul's in-built cynicism against anything new, aligned with his fear of how technology affects human nature. Paul's immediate reaction to any new development would always be, oh yeah? 'The internet is going to change the world? How is it going to change the world?' he demanded of me on countless occasions.

'Well, it already has,' I would argue back.

On this particular occasion, Paul was droning on and on about how crap computers were, how the internet was fucking rubbish, and suddenly I snapped. I was pissed off with him for ruining the evening anyway (see There Is No Drinking).

'For fuck's sake, Paul, shut up,' I said. 'I've heard these whinges a million fucking times.'

'Do you want to go outside?' he simply asked, fixing me with a stare. 'Sort it out.'

'You don't mind technology when it works for you, like in the studio, do you? And no, I don't want to go outside.'

'Let's go outside and talk about it,' he insisted. 'Come on, outside.'

'Oi oi,' said Crowley, 'come on, we're not here to fight.'

'Have a word with him then,' Paul snapped. 'Talk to him, not me.'

I left soon after, found myself walking down a road Paul Weller and I could have been exchanging punches on, and all because the computer had been invented. This is the level where Paul's extreme intolerance can lead to. Once his position is established, he will literally fight to maintain it.

It is striking that in 1978, when computers, mobile phones and the internet were a million miles away, Paul was railing against modern inventions even then. Nearly thirty years on and nothing has changed. In fact, he is growing proud of his intolerance.

Call me a grumpy old man, he told a magazine last year, I don't care. I'm right. You're wrong.

Good album title for him, that.

ELEVEN

"A" Bomb In Wardour Street
(*All Mod Cons*, 1978)

Paul and Violence (Part One)

London has always had a high level of violence. According to certain accounts, the capital's first ever rock'n'roll club, The Two I's, thrived on a menacing atmosphere. In the 1960s, rival Mod gangs regularly fought each other with knives and iron bars. In the late sixties, football violence took off in a major fashion, and that level of violence has sustained itself pretty much ever since. Concerts were not exempt. Punk gigs especially were forever being disrupted by fighting and crowd trouble.

Paul knew all about violence. His school had a major reputation for it, and Woking town on a Friday night was no picnic either, especially if the army boys had come in from nearby Aldershot. But despite asking people outside to settle certain arguments (see In The

Crowd), Paul usually abhorred violence and fighting but, like many of us, he was fascinated by it. I remember one day asking him what he had got up to the night before and him replying that he had watched Stanley Kubrick's *A Clockwork Orange* 'for the millionth time'. Then he added, 'I got to stop watching it,' as if he was deriving some kind of unhealthy pleasure from it. Which he probably was. There is a mean streak in Paul that in part mirrors the film's main character Alex and his ultra violent tendencies. It is one of the reasons he inspires wariness in all close to him.

Part of this may be explained by his roots. Woking was full of boys and men who practised violence for violence's sake. There was no rhyme or reason to their aggression, it was just what they did. You often found yourself running down the road being pursued by a gang for absolutely no reason whatsoever. Woking was that kind of town, and this is the environment Paul grew up in. Note, too, what he said about his 1988 confrontation with Polydor Records head David Munns: 'No one talks to me like that, I'm from Woking and I don't give a fuck.'

I know of only two fights involving Paul. The first was in a Leeds hotel bar with a group of rugby players that ended in a court appearance (at which Paul was immediately acquitted). Jam bassist Bruce Foxton stepped in to help him out, even though the pair of them were completely outnumbered. 'Say what you like about him, I'll always remember him doing that,' Paul told me. This was years after The Jam had broken up and there was bad blood between him and Foxton. The second incident Paul told me about was outside the Marquee one New Year's Eve. He didn't tell me what the fight was about or who it was with, but I do recall him remembering how the white jumper he was wearing that night was totally ruined (see The Peacock Suit).

That incident may have inspired this song: the Marquee, after all, was in Wardour Street. Paul didn't tell. In interviews, he always maintained that it was the disturbing atmosphere at gigs that drove him to write A Bomb. Naturally, he neglected to add that the music of Ray Davies was a massive help in its creation. A Bomb's main riff can be found on a 1976 Kinks song called The Hard Way, while the song's striking musical finale is lifted directly from the middle eight of another Kinks song, Last Of The Steam Powered Trains.

Although A Bomb's imagery is a little bit over the top, particularly the apocalyptic warning at the end, the song can be seen as the first blueprint for his far superior composition Down In The Tube Station At Midnight. A Bomb was one of the first songs written for this landmark album, while Tube Station was one of the last. Paul often worked this way. He told me several times that when it came to writing albums 'the first songs are always the hardest to come by. But once I have them under my belt and I'm happy with them, then the writing becomes easier.'

Despite his musical borrowing, again Weller is able to create a striking song, one that reflected the spirit of those violent times.

TWELVE

Down In The Tube Station At Midnight
(*All Mod Cons*, 1978)

Paul and Violence (Part Two)

This song, released as the second single from the album, was a major breakthrough for The Jam. Even those opposed to Weller's music normally acquiesce when it comes to this record. Weller brought the work into the studio in a very rough form, unsure whether it was worth recording or not; but Bruce Foxton's great bass line, the song's poetic lyrics and the unusual sound and arrangement convinced all of its merit. Musically, no one was sounding like this in 1978.

Although many could point to Weller's retro music inclinations, Jam records always sounded contemporary, always leapt out of the speakers with huge vitality. Yet in terms of the sound they sculpted for this album, Down In The Tube Station stands out even from those songs. It has a unique loose arrangement, a strong emphasis on the vocals, and cutting guitar lines, some of which, the songwriter Dr Robert once told me, are major seventh chords. 'No one was using major sevenths in 1978,' he said, 'no one. That record made all of us musicians go scurrying to the songbook to work out the chords, and that's how I discovered major sevenths.'

Lyrically, the song caught many people's imaginations. Weller's theme, again, is the random nature of violence, so prevalent at that time. His middle-class protagonist descends into a tube station which turns into a living hell when he is viciously attacked by a group of skinheads. They rob him and go off with his front door keys, heading now towards his wife, waiting patiently at home. What makes the story so compelling is Weller's descriptive powers, the best of them located in the small details: the main character buys a ticket from a machine and it comes out as a plum; the dirty steps he walks upon reflect his thoughts; when the first punch arrives he can't help noting the strong smell of alcohol on his attacker's breath.

The song acts itself out as a play. Paul often told me how as a kid he adored watching the BBC's famed *Play for Today* on a Wednesday night. This noted drama series, which began in 1970 and finished in 1984, satisfied Paul's conviction that art should not only entertain but provoke. The series tended to concentrate on gritty contemporary drama from playwrights such as John Osborne, Dennis Potter, Alan Bleasdale, Ken Loach and

Mike Leigh. It was hugely successful, much of Britain eagerly discussing the merits of each play the following morning at work.

Tube Station took this *Play for Today* tradition and placed it in a compelling musical context. This was challenging, commercially successful art that thoroughly explained why even his detractors had to acknowledge Weller's talents. Not all were convinced, though. Famously, the Radio One DJ Tony Blackburn refused to play it on his show as the subject matter was just too depressing. 'Why can't people talk about the good things in life,' he asked, 'like the flowers and the trees?' Recalling Blackburn's advice, Weller recently said, 'Come to think of it, many of my songs these past few years have been about flowers and the trees. So thanks for the advice, Tone.'

THIRTEEN

Thick As Thieves (*Setting Sons*, 1979)

Paul and Friendships (Part Two)

This is a song about friendship, but not mine and Paul's. I was a small pebble in his consciousness when he wrote this. Other people, old friends such as Steve Brookes, Roger Pilling, Dave Waller, maybe even Steve Baker, the ones that called themselves the Clan at school, were on his mind. (Paul had a penchant for naming groups of his friends. When he, his designer Simon Halfon and I hung out a lot together, we were the Three Musketeers.)

Paul's idea for this album was to write a series of linking songs that would tell the story of four close friends driven apart by war. This device would allow him to examine the nature of friendship from several different angles. This song, Burning Sky and Little Boy Soldiers were part of this cycle, but in the end Weller was unable to complete the mission to his satisfaction. (Because Paul ran out of songs, the album ends with a rushed cover version of Holland, Dozier and Holland's *Heatwave*. This recording put Paul and Mick Talbot together in a studio for the first time.) No matter: *Setting Sons* contains much classic Jam music, and is a fine companion to *All Mod Cons*. In later years Weller would say that the album was too slick for his liking, but most people rightly view this and *Cons* as the essence of the band.

Thick As Thieves is an imaginative, bittersweet composition that details the end of a long friendship. Interestingly, after my friendship with Paul ended, he suddenly started to play it live. Although neither of us has ever spoken about what went down between us, this was typical of the man, expressing himself through his music, not conversation.

Paul has enormous pride; he is incredibly headstrong. He believes every decision he makes is the right one. It is imperative, therefore, that he stick to his guns. It is no less than a betrayal of himself to do otherwise. Paul's firm belief is that the move that angered and disappointed me so much was the correct one (he would also have convinced those around him of this fact so as to strengthen his case), and either I accept that or tough luck. In Paul's world, you are either with him or not. There is no in between, it's black and white. Take it, or stay in the trenches.

What kind of friend, then, was Paul? He was the best of friends, and the worst of friends. He was incredibly generous, incredibly mean. He was your most loyal supporter, and your biggest critic. He was the funniest man you knew, and the most miserable. He was the most thoughtful, and the most thoughtless. He was the most perceptive friend, but easily the most pig-headed. Sometimes he was just wonderful to be with, other times you couldn't wait to get home. He could be so interesting, yet so dogmatic. He could be fun, but also an absolute nightmare, especially when drunk (see There Is No Drinking). In all of this, one constant remained: Paul Weller marched to his own drum beat, and that made him forever fascinating, never boring.

After that night in the Wheatsheaf when Paul turned down my request for an interview, I didn't see him again until late 1977, just prior to the release of *The Modern World*. By then he had fallen in love with Gill Price, and you never saw him alone. They literally moved as one. He would sit at a pub table, an arm slung protectively around her. When they walked down the street, they did so with their arms around each other's waists.

He was very quiet then, although when he joined me at the bar he surprised me by expressing real regret at Marc Bolan's recent death in a terrible car accident. I knew enough about Paul by then to know that Bolan's music was not his cup of tea, but he had been on Marc's TV show. 'He was a good pop musician,' he told me. 'In fact, we've just done a pop album, and it's really good.'

But it wasn't. *The Modern World* in no way built on the potential Paul had shown the previous year. I recall going to see the band at Bracknell Sports Centre and it all felt a bit heavy going, a bit dour compared to previous shows I had seen. The tension that had infiltrated the band, due to poor record sales, was now showing on stage. Still, The Jam were given the Friday night headline slot at Reading Festival in August 1978, and at that show the band previewed some of their new album *All Mod Cons*, songs such as Mr Clean and Billy Hunt. That's when I knew they were back on track.

After the gig, Steve Carver and I bunked it backstage, got into the Polydor hospitality tent. I tried to talk to Paul but there was some kerfuffle going on between Gill and the Boomtown Rats, and his attentions were elsewhere. (Instead, Sham 69's Jimmy Pursey sat me down and sang me an impromptu a cappella version of his forthcoming single Hurry Up Harry, which was . . . something. It brings to mind Paul's quote about the lyrics 'we're going down the pub' probably being true for thousands of kids, but he has to aspire to something higher.)

I saw The Jam a couple of times on the tour to promote *All Mod Cons*. By then I was a student at North London Poly in Kentish Town, writing for the student paper and doing small gig reviews for *Melody Maker*. Just prior to the eagerly anticipated release of The Jam's *Setting Sons* album, the band played a secret gig at London's Marquee venue, under the name John's

Boys. Through my Woking connections, I got into that show – the only journalist present – and reviewed it for *MM*. The paper was impressed and sent me on my first feature assignment, to interview The Jam in Manchester. I went with photographer Tom Sheehan. On the way up I told him that there shouldn't be any bother getting Weller to agree to an interview. I knew him, I told Sheehan, he would be fine.

Coincidentally, when we arrived at the hotel, Paul was just coming out of a lift wearing a smart white jacket and jeans. I greeted him, told him I was looking forward to interrogating him. 'That's if I fucking speak to you,' he barked, and then haughtily walked off. My face went crimson. Later, we went down to the bar. There was a whole bunch of journalists present who were also covering the band, including Charles Shaar Murray, whom I nervously eyed. Paul then walked in, came straight over to me. I tensed myself, but instantly he was polite and friendly and very warm. It was his way of apologizing for his earlier behaviour. The next day we did the interview, and I went home and wrote the piece, which was extremely complimentary.

The following week, I saw Paul at the Rainbow Theatre, Finsbury Park. The venue was near where I lived so I sauntered down in the afternoon to see if I could get into the soundcheck. About a hundred young Jam fans were eagerly grouped around the stage door when I arrived. Paul's minder, Kenny Wheeler, was guarding the entrance. Luckily, he recognized me and let me through. I walked into the auditorium. Paul was sitting in the stalls, watching the support band soundcheck. I went over, greeted him. He had on a striking, beautiful green suede jacket. We chit-chatted, then I asked him what he thought of my article.

'Nah, didn't like it,' he said, sniffily.

Paul was always up front with his opinions. He never held back. Sometimes it was quite endearing; other times he made you burn with humiliation and anger. He offered no explanation as to why he didn't like my piece, though he did say he liked it better than the recent *NME* interview. This wasn't surprising. Paul Morley, not a fan, had written it, and in doing so had severely annoyed the young Weller. Among other crimes, I recall Paul being really scathing about Morley likening him to a caged tiger. 'Fucking animal, am I?' he seethed.

I thought Morley was spot on. Paul was a restless ball of nerves and tension. The man could never stay still. He was always moving, always adjusting his clothes, always fidgeting: fiddling with his jacket sleeves, pulling on his socks, playing with his ciggy, playing with his hair. I did not point this out. Paul had a knack of expressing his opinion so strongly it became crystal clear that there was no point whatsoever in any further discussion.

Not long after that, Paul called me at the *Melody Maker*'s offices. Did I fancy going for a drink that night? I did, and from then on we began hanging out. A couple of weeks later I went down to Woking to see him. He was visiting the family home on Balmoral Drive, Maybury. We went to a local pub, got merry. I stayed the night. In the morning, his gran made us a breakfast of boiled egg and toast. Paul immediately took his out into the garden to eat. I soon understood why. One, his hero Steve Marriott used to eat in the garden; two, I spent the whole meal being asked by his gran whether I was Jewish or not. After all, she kept saying, I did have quite a big nose.

There was much that bonded Paul and me, much we had in common. Music was the obvious starting point (see Walls Come Tumbling Down), and clothes (see The Peacock Suit). Then there were the books and writers we both gravitated to. Paul's were mainly British: Orwell, Wilde, Tressell, the playwright Tony Marchant. (Paul's later solo song The Strange Museum was based on Tony's play *The Attractions* which Paul and I saw in London.) A big book for both of us was *Absolute Beginners* by Colin MacInnes. In fact, after I read it I agitated Paul to buy the rights to it. He didn't as we both presumed – wrongly, as it turned out – that they would be prohibitively expensive (see Have You Ever Had It Blue?). Unsurprisingly, Paul devoured all good material that was sixties-related: books on clothes and music, histories of recording studios, biographies of his favourite artists. Yet you couldn't pin him down. I read Shane McGowan's book *A Drink With Shane McGowan*, and loved it. 'You got to read this,' I said. He handed it back a week later. 'Too much swearing,' the softly and extremely well-spoken Weller opined.

In film and television, as well, we generally agreed. Paul was a huge fan of classic British comedies such as

Hancock's Half Hour and *Steptoe and Son*, and anything by Peter Cook and Dudley Moore. He loved films, and great TV dramas. Jeremy Brett as Sherlock Holmes springs to mind, as do *Kes*, *Cathy Come Home*, the Stephen Frears Joe Orton biog *Prick Up Your Ears*, a 1969 film called *Bronco Bullfrog* which featured a gaggle of East End kids bouncing around in crombies and button-down shirts, Ealing comedies such as *Passport to Pimlico* or *The Ladykillers*, and, of course, *A Clockwork Orange*. Both of us loved Mike Leigh's film *Meantime*. Years ago we met one of the actors in it, Phil Daniels, at a National Film Theatre event. Paul and I spent the whole night calling him 'muppet', the term he uses heavily in the film. I don't think Daniels got it, or if he did he masked his boredom very well.

Paul's tastes always tended towards the British. When the American comedy show *Cheers* began, Simon Halfon and I quickly became huge fans. We urged Paul to watch it. He did so, and to our great surprise said he really disliked it.

'Why?' I asked.

'Because the lighting was too dark,' he stated.

Frazier, *Seinfeld*, *Curb Your Enthusiasm* – all passed him by. Too intellectual, too much word play for Paul – he liked his comedy to be more robust, more earthy, more *Carry On*. He was a great fan of British cinema, American too, but usually the populists such as Steven Spielberg. I remember pushing him to watch Martin Scorsese's great Italian-American film *Mean Streets*, if only because at the film's start Robert de Niro, in his leather jacket and trilby hat, looks just like Paul. Finally, he watched it. And?

'Couldn't understand a fucking word they were saying.'

(When I gave him a copy of Scorsese's *Raging Bull* for Christmas one year, Paul thought I was winding him up. I wasn't. I was sending him signals, wanting him to take heed of the film's ending . . .)

But there were other factors that brought us together. We had ambition and drive in our blood. Both of us had escaped our backgrounds, and sought to realize cherished dreams. Success was crucial, but on our terms, not theirs. (In daydreams, I saw us as a team, bank robbers on a caper, coming to London to make our names, Paul with music, me with words.) We disliked unfairness, the English class system. Both of us suffered class prejudice, class discrimination, although I took much more than Paul ever did simply because of the profession I work in. In the 1980s, the Thatcher era, we became politically committed, left wing through and through. Party politics killed that in us, but it didn't kill our sense of injustice.

The differences between us were few, but they were marked. Paul was far more confident than me. My childhood was dark, horrible; it filled me with great self loathing, left me with low self-esteem. Paul was the opposite. His upbringing took place in the bosom of a truly loving family. From day one, he felt loved, special. He once told me that he used to wake up every day and with a shiver of anticipation think, 'I wonder what the world has in store for me today?' I used to wake up and think, 'Please God, just get me through the day.'

Paul's greatest gift, then, was to help rebuild my confidence. He couldn't change my past, but he could do something about my future. He regularly told me that I was a good writer, and he did so until the day I finally believed it. He consistently encouraged me, was forever suggesting ideas for articles, books, films. Once, when my daughter was being christened, I told him I was thinking of not going as her mum and I were in a bad space. He told me to get round to his and that we were going, no matter what. He put me in his car, he drove me to that church, and he stood firm beside me at the ceremony. Paul had great generosity of spirit, and it was that quality in him I prized above all. He never shirked from criticizing me, but he was just as quick to praise. Like Muhammad Ali before him, Paul instinctively understood the power of positive thinking. His next record was always going to be the best ever made, the next gig the most wonderful. Paul installed that way of thinking in me – again, priceless.

Contrary to his public persona, Paul has a great sense of humour. He loved friendly banter (as long as it didn't go too far), mickey taking, clever wordplay, and puns. Neil Tennant of the Pet Shop Boys was Neil by mouth; Bono was Bonzo; George Michael didn't have a sense of houmos. And so on. He loved the idiosyncratic nature of others. Once we met a Geordie guy in a bar, got talking to him. He told us Newcastle girls were the best in the country 'because they wear skirts up to here', and he viciously jabbed at the top of his thigh. The observation quickly became a saying between us.

'Did you like that girl?'

'No.'

'Why not?'

'Didn't have her skirt up to here, man.'

FOURTEEN

Private Hell (*Setting Sons*, 1979)

Paul and Women

According to an interview he granted the now defunct *Watch* magazine in 2002, Paul locked himself into an office at Nomis Rehearsal Studios to write two more songs needed to complete the fourth Jam album. He had a guitar, a desk and a phone. He got in at ten in the morning and worked office hours until he had written the required quota. Paul loved this kind of pressure. Days to go before the album has to be finished and more songs needed. And just when you thought he had missed the boat, there's Weller with the goods, the golden boy again.

One of the songs he wrote in this office was the album's opening track, Girl On The Phone – one of the few songs in existence to use the phrase 'size of my cock'. The second song was Private Hell. Good song, this, and another demonstration of Paul's lyrical abilities, his way with detail, his way of getting into people's minds, and his love of the Wilko Johnson guitar style and The Beatles' Dr Robert riff. I once told the Blow Monkeys' Dr Robert that his song Lucifer's Friend reminded me too much of the Jam song But I'm Different Now. Robert told Paul this, who replied, 'That's funny, because for But I'm Different Now I nicked the riff from that Beatles song Dr Robert.'

This song describes the inner turmoil of a mother left alone to struggle with the passing of time and her beauty, the dreams she never fulfilled, the bored unsympathetic husband, the crushing mundanity of life and the 'Valium haze' she loses herself in to cope with the 'private hell' she experiences every day. Paul hasn't often written from a female point of view, but when he does, the results can be quite impressive – The Butterfly Collector, A Woman's Song, for example.

Furthermore, the song does not state the woman's class. However, the line about her son Edward 'who is still at college, you send him letters which he doesn't acknowledge' would suggest that Paul is writing about someone who is at least lower middle class. And that was quite a step for him.

FIFTEEN

Saturday's Kids (*Setting Sons*, 1979)

Paul and his Woking Songs (Part One)

This was the kind of song that made The Jam unique. Paul wrote it as a poem which he published in the *All Mod Cons* songbook. No one was writing about such people, the council estate kids with their factory jobs, their routine lives of hard work and hard play, their fashions, their rites and rituals. Paul Weller did. He had wanted punk to be a genuine working-class movement, and in his eyes it hadn't been. He now set out to chronicle the lives of his contemporaries and in doing so stand up for them. The Saturday kids were his people, the ones he had grown up with, gone to school with, fought and played with; these were the people he knew back to front, the ones, in fact, who now bought his records and worshipped him so. He knew their ways intimately.

A year of my teenage Saturdays are summed up in the first verse of this song. It's all there in black and white: meet at the Albion pub midday, drink till afternoon closing time, off to the local Light A Bite, heady on alcohol, think the waitresses in their tight nylon uniforms and little white socks incredibly erotic, ask for tea and a date, get rebuffed, look for the football scores (the Spurs, of course!) and go home to prepare for the night.

I remember Paul once remarking to me, 'I don't know why they make such a fuss about my lyrics. Everyone does, but all I am doing is writing about what I see around me.'

Ah, but if only it were that easy, then we would all be at it. Weller has great observational powers, and knows the value of the telling detail. He sings about the wallpaper lives, the dipping into silver paper, the inevitable marriage, the baby on the way. The vision is hard-edged, realistic, as all Weller's songs tended to be when addressing such issues.

Moreover, this song lifts the lid on a set of attitudes and routines music rarely reflects, and accounts for Weller's high standing among many. I have no idea if the Saturday kids still live the same way, but this is their first manifesto, enshrined for ever.

SIXTEEN

Going Underground (Single, 1980)

Paul and Fame (Part Two)

Funny story. It was summer, the early eighties, maybe 1983 or 1984. Paul was definitely in The Style Council by then. It was midweek, and the pair of us had just been for dinner at Kettner's restaurant on Romilly Street, Soho. Paul was wearing a bright yellow jersey. We stood by Cambridge Circus looking for cabs. None was currently available. As we looked in vain, both of us noted two guys staring at us from across the street. I took them to be fans, but when we walked down Shaftesbury Avenue the pair followed us.

'Paul,' I said, 'those guys—'

'Yeah, I know, they're following us. Keep walking.'

We walked on, came to a building on our right that was under renovation. Paul said, 'Wait here. If they start anything, grab those planks down there.'

We stopped, looked around. The guys were walking purposefully towards us, staring quite blatantly. I thought, Here we go, and prepared myself. But before I could do anything, one of them reached into his pocket, pulled out a small black wallet, and opened it.

'Police!' he barked, shoving the badge into Paul's face. 'What's your name?'

'Paul.'

'Paul what?'

'Paul Weller.'

He stopped for a second, then he turned to his mate. 'I fucking told you it was him, didn't I? We were only playing Going Underground in the canteen last night. Up on the tables, we were.' Then he started singing: 'Going underground, going underground . . .'

Paul smiled, said, 'We saw you looking at us across the street.'

'Yeah, we had a report of someone wearing a yellow jersey trying to steal cars, that's why we were checking you out.' Pause. 'Hey, it wasn't you, was it?'

Going Underground was the record that told the world just how big The Jam had become. Two years earlier they had been close to destruction. Now, with advance orders of 200,000 copies sending this song straight to number one (consider that today you can actually sell two thousand copies and go top forty), The Jam had become something like a phenomenon.

Such was the hysteria around the band, and Paul in particular, is it not possible to see Weller's desire to exist underground as the reaction of a shy man to the huge attention the world now focused on him? The song details absurdities, a world where rockets and guns are more important than kidney machines, where fascism is on the rise, where people accept and never challenge. These were typical Weller concerns at the time, reflecting his great unease at the modern world. His poetic pronouncements, his sullen persona, his manifest anger at injustice, his way with melody and noise, and sound and arrangements, his image, his hard-edged but poetic lyrics, all of this made Paul a true man of the people.

Yet he was not particularly cut out for such acclaim. As an artist he was inward-looking, and in those days he took everything very, very seriously. Many were the times he would snap at people if he found fault with their conversation. One time in a café in Hanover Square, Gary Crowley was talking about some of the guests he had interviewed on his Capital Radio show. Paul remained quiet until suddenly he brought his fist down on the table, stood up, angrily said to Crowley, 'If I didn't like you so much, Gary, I would kick your head in,' and stormed off, leaving us to wonder what the hell had just happened.

Records such as this one gave him the dubious title of Spokesman for a Generation, a meaningless label he pushed aside at every opportunity. It was a mantle he would bear for another two years, and then he would cast it aside for ever and gleefully throw himself upon the winds of fate and discovery.

Although The Jam hammered this record in most of their live sets, after their demise it was over twenty years before Paul played it again, one time, at a radio show performance in West London. Grown men were not seen to cry, they were seen to jump on one another's shoulders and sing and shout, for in these three and something minutes they heard strong echoes of their youth coming right back at them again.

SEVENTEEN

Start! (Single, 1980)

Paul and Communication

Paul Weller has always refused to rest on his laurels, to take the easy road. This number one single from September 1980 is a massive case in point. The four preceding singles to Start! were as follows: Going Underground, The Eton Rifles, When You're Young, and Strange Town. Put together, these four recordings work roughly according to the same highly successful blueprint. Each begins with a dramatic intro, features vocals that are either very clipped (Underground) or start off relaxed but quickly speed up, boasts a catchy chorus, has the same large sound, and obeys Keith Richards' dictum that for singles to truly work, something new has to happen every ten seconds. Paul could quite easily have chosen to milk this musical vein incessantly but instead he chose to follow up his biggest single to date with a brand-new approach.

At the time, Weller said that the song's main influence was *Off The Wall*, the great debut solo album from Michael Jackson. Certainly, this is by far the 'danciest' of Jam tracks, uniquely mixing touches of funk with psychedelic and pop to create a song whose quality is still somewhat underestimated, I feel. Through its very taut musical nature, immediate attention is drawn to its bass line, obviously taken from the Beatles song *Taxman*. But there is much more to it than mere lifting. There is a cutting guitar solo, echoey backing vocals, tight drum rhythms, touches of psychedelia, and direct lyrics, aimed at the band's legions of fans and designed to alleviate the pressure surrounding Paul.

In 1980, the world The Jam operated in was one where communication channels were highly restrictive. This was a world where to appear on television was actually an event, an achievement, not the everyday occurrence it is today. ITV, BBC1 and BBC2 were the only television channels available. Apart from the various one-offs that had sprung up in the wake of punk – *Something Else*, *So It Goes*, which had only been given limited runs – the two main music shows were *Top of the Pops* and *The Old Grey Whistle Test*. You needed chart success for one, good credibility for the other. The Jam had both, and they appeared many times on the former and once on the latter.

Radiowise, there was only Radio One, a very conservative pop station whose shows were hosted by safe and actually quite eccentric DJs. The Jam's huge popularity demanded airplay and attention. You could not imagine any Radio One DJ, apart from one or two, actively liking The Jam, in the way you can today. This is why the music press, the *NME* in particular, was so important: it was the only intelligent musical forum for artists such as Paul to discuss their views and opinions, to reveal themselves. These conditions suited Paul. The fewer people badgering him for interviews, the fewer people trying to break down the cool, hard persona that fronted the band, the better. As one fan noted to me once, 'I didn't even really know how Paul spoke as such until I saw him being interviewed in 1982 on Brighton Pier about the end of The Jam.'

As communication with his audience was so restrictive, Paul insisted on an open-door policy for his fans at soundchecks, and later backstage after the shows. Even then, communication was difficult. 'I've seen people come in here shaking,' he once said of fans about to be brought into his dressing room. Start! puts a positive spin on these matters, arguing that 'even if we only talk for two minutes it will be a start.'

Paul always sought to treat his fans with respect, but some unnerved him, especially those whose devotion to him seemed to signal a deeper malaise. 'I'm sure,' he once mused, looking at a group of fans standing outside a venue door, 'one of them will stab me one day.' Such are the concerns of the well known.

EIGHTEEN

Liza Radley (B Side of Start! 1980)

Paul and Isolation in Woking

One of The Jam's greatest songs, and another inspired by Weller's Woking experiences. In the same way that the Ray Davies song Two Sisters is actually about the writer and his brother, it is very tempting to see Paul as Liza Radley, the small town's misfit, the one who says very little but is acutely aware of all around, the one people think is a bit weird, just as I did when he came into my consciousness as a fully fledged Mod in the year of the soul boy, 1975. Paul must have got a re-action from many in Woking simply because of his individuality. No one I knew rode a scooter around town and dressed himself in Mod clothes. Paul was a one-off, and would have felt the disparity between him-self and his peers just as keenly as Liza Radley does in this song. Like her, Paul said little, but in his own room probably expressed in words (and maybe tears) his thoughts on their lives. The lyrics are bright and concise, and the melody is as haunting as the song's central character.

This is Paul's most revealing song from this period, opening up the loneliness of the individual for all to see. The album he released in November 1980, *Sound Affects*, carried little insight into his character. In contrast, it was marked by Weller's attempt to give The Jam a new direction both musically and lyrically. Out went the character-driven songs, the words became dreamier, less harsh, less open, and the sound was stripped of all the slickness that he believed had ruined *Setting Sons*. But this song is simple, straightforward and quite affecting, probably because when Paul thought of Liza Radley he actually saw himself.

NINETEEN

That's Entertainment
(*Sound Affects*, 1980)

Paul and Poetry

When considering his achievements, Paul often wavered between two contradictory viewpoints. Sometimes, in a bullish mood, he firmly stated that his success was down to one fact alone, that he had worked fucking hard for everything that came his way, and although admittedly you might need a bit of luck here and there, his success was down to him and him alone. On other occasions a more spiritual side emerged. He had been put on this earth to make music, and he was grateful to have been chosen for such a task.

When you consider the circumstances that led to the writing of this song, you might think both points of view have great validity.

By 1979, Paul had set aside some of his earnings to set up a publishing company he named Riot Stories. He was keen to publish the work of his good friend Dave Waller (see Man Of Great Promise) as well as encourage young poets by featuring their work in anthologies. He put out a call for work to be sent to him, and one poem in particular caught his eye. It was written by a lad called Paul Drew, and was called Entertainment. This is the work, in full.

A dead body on the hour, one, six nine or ten – that's
  entertainment
a rape before the horlicks, a simulated orgasm before the
  Bovril –
NOTHING IS FUNNY ANYMORE
That's entertainment
murder with a point or without a point while off spring
  throw toys at each other
Poison in the air you laugh with the comedians know
  they are watching
Elite defeat your thought – CRYPTIC CRYPTIC
Tea or coffee, gonoreah, cream bun, cambodia,
  doughnut, syphilis,
the daily express, the british movement, marks and
  spencers, harrisburg,
Degree in geography, cancer, E.L.O., UDA
It's all the same isn't it
Murphy's war and the Vietnam war, it's all the same
  that's entertainment

You can see why Paul was attracted to the poem. It is quite Welleresque, the way it sarcastically contrasts the well-known title of a middle-of-the-road film with raw, disturbing images. Paul immediately saw the possibilities this poem presented, Drew's use of scattershot images in particular exciting him. He quickly began work on his own version. This impulse to rework the world was a consistent thread in Paul's character. Even outside music he was the same, always making suggestions, always looking to bend things to his way of thinking. 'I like your haircut, but why don't you do it like this next time?' he would say to me. Or, 'Good shoes, but the soles could be better.'

Using the same meter and technique, plus the title, of Drew's original, Paul created a set of his own images which, it has to be said, are so much stronger than Drew's. Weller's words, like his images, are random. They are raw – 'a kick in the balls' – mundane – 'feeding ducks in the park and thinking about your holidays' – and beautifully poetic: the 'two lovers missing the tranquillity of solitude', the sentence everyone picks up on. Many of them presented themselves to Paul at the time of writing, such as the police car hurtling past his flat which had damp walls and sometimes shook to the sound of a band rehearsing nearby.

In a recent Radio Two documentary, Paul gave the idea that he wrote the words to this song while he was drunk, and that the music was created a week later when sober. However, I recall him telling me that he wrote the *music* while drunk in the tiny hallway of his Pimlico flat, playing his guitar softly so as not to wake either Gill or the neighbours. One thing is for sure, he is absolutely correct when he states that 'the chords are very simple. There are only four of them. The main flow of the song are the words really and the music is almost secondary to it.'

The music, in fact, is very reminiscent of a chord sequence he had already used, for his song When You're Young. Played on an acoustic, these chords sound a mile away from that explosive single. They carry echoes of George Harrison's song My Sweet Lord, which in turn had been 'inspired' by The Chiffons' song He's So Fine.

Within ten minutes or so, Weller had under his belt a song that would make him a lot of moolah. It was duly recorded for the *Sound Affects* album, the song ending what in those days was quaintly known as side one of the record. Demands quickly came from both his record company and, unusually, his audience for it to be released as a single. Paul, of course, refused to sanction its release. Too obvious, for at the time Start! as a single excited him far more. A German import single of That's Entertainment eventually found its way into this country as a 45, and it entered the charts as one of the highest-selling import singles ever. A video was also shot, Weller obviously halfway to alcohol paradise, swaying on a stool and playing the song with verve and energy, Bruce and Rick in their normal positions.

The song lies at the very heart of The Jam's canon. It has featured on a million Jam compilations and is still played to this day by Paul, who recognizes its great strengths. It has endured, truly stood the test of time. God bless you, wherever you are, Paul said to Paul Drew during the Radio Two documentary. But on this occasion one feels God blessed two Pauls.

TWENTY

Happy Together (*The Gift*, 1982)

Paul and Gill

This was the first song written for *The Gift*, an album Weller tried desperately hard to make his finest to date. Instead, it proved to be his band's swansong.

The song's lyrics pertain to his relationship with his girlfriend at the time, Gill Price. Weller met Gill at a Jam gig in 1978. They fell for each other instantly, but the relationship was always highly volatile in nature. When I began hanging out with Paul, it was actually quite shocking to witness just how volatile things could get. Many was the time an evening would end with the pair arguing like crazy, taking separate cabs screaming back to their Pimlico flat, where the fight would continue.

Gill was certainly an individual. She was a lover of 1920s films, 1920s style. She even had her hair styled after Louise Brooks, a famous actress from the 1920s.

She also, like her boyfriend, had a wicked tongue on her which cut quickly to the bone. At a party once, I wore a new pinstripe jacket. I asked her what she thought of it. Gill said with a perfect sneer, 'you look like you're in the fucking *Sweeney*.' That was one of her nicer comments.

The pair argued continually, and the fights were not just verbal. One time Paul had to go to hospital after he brought a china cup down on his own head in frustration during an argument. Once I even saw the pair end up wrestling on the pavement outside the ICA, Gill clawing away at Paul, Paul trying to avoid her nails. Madness.

I remember meeting Paul and Gill at a bar in St Christopher's Place one night. It was the early eighties. A new club playing psychedelic music had opened up on nearby Kingleigh Street. Gill wanted to go. Paul didn't. You could see his point: whatever club he went to, it was odds on he was going to draw massive attention to himself, a nightmare scenario for the shy boy about town. Gill didn't care. She spent hours wearing him down, trying to get Paul to change his mind, the conversation painful and distracting. Eventually, Paul gave in. 'OK,' he said in conciliatory tones, 'finish these drinks and we'll go there.'

Thank God that's over, I thought. Stupidly.

Gill put her glass down, looked at him with drunken eyes and said, 'It's like living with a fucking monk, living with you.'

'What did you fucking call me?'

Evening over, two cabs called.

It was a mad relationship, one that left everyone baffled. Why did Paul put up with it? He later explained his devotion to Gill by stating that he thought all relationships were like his, that the man and the woman fought each other all the time. His parents might have provided ammunition for that notion: they often snapped away at each other in public, albeit good-naturedly. But it was never to the level of bad-temperedness Paul and Gill seemed to thrive on.

'Any type of Jam love song,' Paul said at the time, 'I always write from my own personal relationship, otherwise to me love songs don't mean anything unless there's some kind of truth behind it. So it is kind of sarcastic because me and my girlfriend are always arguing, we are always so unhappy . . .' Funny how Paul, the self-centred man of pleasure, suffered so long within a relationship where happiness was just a fleeting smile at best. It was as if he had accepted it as a cross he must bear. His quick temper and her acid tongue were a marriage made in a caged kick-boxing ring, and it couldn't continue, it had to burn itself out, which it did in the early eighties. But the link between happiness and his main relationship is one that popped up again many years later (see Remember How We Started).

TWENTY-ONE

Ghosts (*The Gift*, 1982)

Paul and Personal Freedom

In his book *Music and Imagination*, you will recall, the composer Aaron Copland asks why the creative impulse is never satisfied. He answers the question himself: because without that there is no outlet for the artist's numerous and varied emotions. I would add the word 'characters' to Copland's explanation, and this song is a massive case in point.

Paul's personality at this stage of his life was inward, restrictive, dour even. So conscious was he of not disappointing his audience, so conscious was he of not putting a foot wrong, he maintained a strict twenty-four-hour vigil on himself. He was naturally shy, naturally secretive. You could sit in silence for hours with this man. Therefore, to write a song exhorting the listener to open yourself up, to throw caution to the wind, to take heed of nothing but your own inner self, not to worry about other people, to reveal your true self to the world, and to deliver this message in such a warm and engaging manner, felt awfully strange coming from such a tension-filled young man. This is why the artist, who feels such a wide variety of emotions and impulses but is unable to articulate them in words, needs to adopt different personas so that he can do so in music. In other words, in writing and performing the song he must become a certain character which then allows him to successfully transmit his ideas and visions. 'His true identity is in his work,' wrote Anthony Storr in *The Dynamics of Creation*, 'and what he presents to the world in social situations is either a false persona or less than half of himself.'

Frankly, in a police line-up one would never have chosen Paul as the author of this song. He was far too uptight at this point in his life. Yet reaching within himself, and using music to communicate, he brought forth a great message for all. This gently insistent beat ballad reflects a side of Paul that is highly personable, and warm, extremely warm. The message is 'to thine own self be true', an idea that Paul would explore more fully in his next band. Within the context of The Jam, however, this song is a surprise, and a welcome one at that.

TWENTY-TWO

Town Called Malice (*The Gift*, 1982)

Paul and his Woking Songs (Part Two)

Heavily chastised on its release for its use of the bass line from the Supremes song You Can't Hurry Love (written by Holland, Dozier and Holland in 1966), Town Called Malice remains a key song in Weller's career. He was given four songs to perform at the Brit Awards in 2006, and Malice was the one he chose to represent his work with The Jam. His decision made absolute sense. Malice carries all the classic hallmarks of a Jam composition. There is the use of a well-known phrase for the song's title – after the best-selling novel *A Town Like Alice* by Nevil Shute – the clear nod towards the musical source that was inspiring him at the time of the song's creation – sixties American r'n'b music – and then there are the lyrics, based in gritty realism but elevated by the sheer force of his poetry.

Paul wrote the song at the old Air Studios on Oxford Street when he was recording The Jam's final album *The Gift* in the latter months of 1981. The lyrics came first. Once they were written, he began playing his guitar until he hit upon the appropriate music. On its release in February 1982, he told the *Melody Maker*, 'I always wanted to do a song with that Motown beat, like Madness have done with Embarrassment [single, November 1980]. That was great, and I've always wanted to do something with that rhythm.' At the time, strangely enough, Paul did not rate the lyrics to Malice as highly as he did some of the other songs he had written. 'To me,' he stated in *Melody Maker*, 'it doesn't come up to the standard of the other songs lyrically.' He would soon change his mind.

The song was based on Woking, where Weller lived until the age of nineteen. Variously described as 'an Essex town that somehow ended up in Surrey' or 'the town that likes to think it's in London', Woking has acted as both carrot and stick to Weller throughout his whole life. For many, it felt like the town was yearning to be part of London's hinterland but was never quite grown up enough to manage it. Weller would grow to despise its small-town ways, its pettiness and un-ambitious nature. Woking was a prison; London, true liberation. Yet ironically it was Woking, its people, its culture and its location, that would act as major inspiration for so many of his songs.

In 1978, after a spell in London which nearly ended with The Jam's extinction, it was to Woking that Weller retreated to write the breakthrough Jam album *All Mod Cons*. In the eighties he stayed away, but in the 1990s he again used Woking as a creative source and wrote his comeback single Uh Uh Oh Yeh, detailing his experiences on revisiting the town. He bought properties in Send and, later on, Ripley, two villages just outside Woking. He lived in Ripley for quite some time until London called him back again. He also bought Black Barn Studios in Ripley in the mid 1990s which to this day acts as the centre of his operations, containing both office and recording studio.

Today, Woking is a sprawling mess of high-rise office blocks and impersonal shopping malls. It has expanded dramatically. But in Paul's time it was a small town that contained a high street, two significant nightclubs (the Atalanta and Michael's), a working men's club, two cinemas, two record shops, a police station, a few pubs and a few schools. It may not have been a big town, but it was, as we have seen, a tough town, violence forever simmering beneath its skin. Teenagers drank in pubs such as the Albion, the Cricketers, the Bird In Hand, the Red House, and then spilled on to midnight streets, spoiling for a fight. Anyone and everyone was a target. You did well to get home unscathed in Woking, you really did. Weller abhorred violence, but he witnessed his fair share of it at places such as Knaphill Disco, Woking Football Club, the Atalanta and his school, Sheerwater Secondary. Sheerwater and Woking taught Weller street smarts, and he was proud to wear those credentials on his sleeve throughout his life, like a badge of courage. To abandon them would, in his eyes, be an act of class betrayal, the actions of 'a pussy'.

Woking was also a town of extremes, rich areas such as Hook Heath to its north, sprawling council estates to the south. It was highly multicultural, too. A large Asian population was to be found south of the train station. Woking was, in fact, home to the first mosque in the UK, located on Oriental Road, where Paul's mum Ann worked as a cleaner for a couple of years. At weekends, the few Indian restaurants which had opened up in town served curry and ducked the racist epithets thrown at them by the young drunks. 'Oi, Gunga Din,' I remember hearing once, 'where are my fucking poppadoms?' Down by Goldsworth Road, the Italians congregated. They too ran restaurants, hairdressing and landscape gardening businesses as well. Catholic schools and churches were built to accommodate them, and in 1985 two major Mafia bosses were arrested in their Woking homes.

Paul himself grew up on Stanley Road, just to the south of the main town, in a tiny house with an outside toilet. His father John was a builder by trade but also a man for all seasons – a cab driver, a bricklayer, a handyman. He was in and out of work on a regular basis and would resort to all kinds of activities to keep bread on the table – hence the song's lyric about either cutting down on beer or the kid's new gear, and that being a massive decision in this town called malice. Paul's highly developed sense of injustice, which would sear through many Jam and Style Council songs, was first sown in Woking. He revelled in working-class culture but railed against the system that created it. Woking would make him a socialist, a position he was heading for politically at the time of this song's release.

The lyrics to Town Called Malice carry many vivid images. There is the milk dairy which once stood on Goldsworth Road where Weller imagines the rows of disused milk floats standing empty (he likes to use the metaphor of inactive vehicles to suggest decay – see Wild Wood), and in front of it he sees a hundred lonely house-wives clutching empty milk bottles to their hearts, like a Busby Berkeley musical that can't afford itself. Later on there is the classic line pertaining to a whole street's belief in Sunday's roast beef, and you can just feel the young artist's frustration as he recalls the mundane conversation that surrounded him at the time. Here he is, the earnest teenager desperately seeking answers to life's deepest mysteries, and all he is being told is what he's having for dinner. No wonder he yearned for London, a city where the young are just as important as the old.

As in most Jam songs, there has to be a call to arms. As the music builds towards the song's glorious finale, Paul switches from description to prescription and declares how it is up to us and him to put some joy back into the town of malice. As he does so, Weller's passion for r'n'b music shines through, especially in his vocal, which reaches the heights at the end.

The song entered the charts at number one. On the day that news broke, Paul was on a week-long break taken with his father, John, tour manager Kenny Wheeler and me. The four of us were travelling the English countryside, visiting castles. The main point of conversation from day one centred on what position Town Called Malice would enter in the charts. As Paul had taken most of the preceding year off, the song's chart position would give the clearest indicator yet of lost ground. Given the fanaticism of their fan base, it was obvious to most of us that the single would go to number one; but complacency was never tolerated within the Jam camp. Plus, to speculate endlessly on the single's fate was a great way to build tension and keep things interesting.

When the news broke of the song's impending success, we were in the bar of some hotel. I recall Paul saying, 'If the song changes some people's minds, that's all I care about.' Then he took another sip of orange juice. This was the Paul Weller of The Jam. It was not in his nature to crack open the champagne, find the dolly birds. That was inexcusable decadence, a symptom of the rotting rock culture he actively opposed. Paul was the moral revolutionary, the man whose purity and strength of vision would overturn the odds for all those who followed him (and who, incidentally, would have despised the Paul Weller of today). Music was his weapon, and songs such as Malice were his call to arms.

I remember also discovering on that trip just how important music was to him. The next day I went out early for a walk and when I got back to my room there were two or three messages on my phone from Paul saying he had to see me about something really important.

I began speculating about what he wanted. The night before we had stayed in his room, listening to music, generally chatting. I was very shy then, very nervous of expressing opinion, so I had surprised myself by telling him that I didn't think The Jam were going to last. My reason was clear: *The Gift* had proved that he would need an urgent overhaul if he was to follow his dream of making The Jam a *soulful* agit-prop band. Something would have to give. He just looked away from me, refusing, I thought, to debate the subject. I thought, Uh oh, overstepped the mark there. So I thought that maybe now he wanted to continue the discussion, maybe even express his dislike for my presumptions. Or maybe he had bigger issues pressing down on him. Maybe he wanted to talk about Gill, or maybe something terrible had happened while we had been away. Either way, from the tone of his voice, I figured it was something really earth-shattering.

I went to his room, knocked on the door.

Paul opened it. 'Ah,' he said, 'been looking for you. Come in, come in. I got to know something.'

Here we go.

He went over to the Dansette record player that was sat on the floor.

'I got this single the other day,' he unexpectedly announced, placing a platter on the turntable and lifting the needle on to it. The record started. 'Now, do you think that's General Johnson from Chairmen of the Board on lead vocals moonlighting, or is that someone different?'

A video for Town Called Malice was shot in a London studio. As with most Jam videos, it is performance-based, with Weller bringing in an organ player (wearing white gloves) and a three-piece horn section. This was the signal of his intention to follow a much wider r'n'b remit – a decision that would lead him to break up The Jam. For all their power and energy – and no disrespect – I thought Bruce Foxton and Rick Buckler lacked the subtlety demanded by this music. Duck Dunn and Al Jackson (Booker T and the MGs' bassist and drummer respectively) they were not. Even so, the next few months would be spent trying to emulate the skill and sound of American r'n'b, but within a pop punk frame-work. Covers such as Edwin Starr's War and The Chi-Lites' Stoned Out Of My Mind would be recorded. All would prove fruitless, hastening Weller's resolve to split the band at the height of their success.

Malice stayed at number one for three weeks and sold over 300,000 copies. It was later used in two films, *Billy Elliot* (2000) and *The Matador* (2006). It was the former's huge success and judicious use of the song that helped give Malice a new lease of life.

By then, secure now in his solo career, Paul had allowed himself to look backwards and widen his song selection. He had been asked to check the tape of a Jam compilation called *Extras*. While listening to that tape,

Paul rediscovered songs he hadn't heard or played in thirteen years. Malice was chosen early on to be included in his live set. At first he played it acoustically before switching to a full-on band performance. In the documentary *Highlights and Hangups*, he argues that on acoustic guitar alone, without the distracting Motown bass riff, the song's depth and talent shine through. The song remains in his set, and is often used as the rousing closing song. Its classic musical qualities have withstood time and proved Weller's point beyond doubt that great songs live for ever.

All you have to do is write them.

TWENTY-THREE

Just Who Is The 5 O'Clock Hero?
(*The Gift*, 1982)

Paul and Politics (Part One)

Paul Weller's public political life began in 1977 when he told the *NME* he would be voting Conservative. He would spend the next thirty years regretting that statement. Just two years later he was telling *Jamming* fanzine, 'I don't really wanna talk about politics, I'm not clever enough.'

Literature, poetry in particular, would change his mind. Riot Stories, the publishing company Paul set up in 1979, had published two poetry anthologies, one by his friend Dave Waller, *Notes From Hostile Street*, and another a collection of unpublished young authors entitled *Mixed Up, Shook Up*. Paul's love of poetry also led him to the work of Percy Bysshe Shelley, whose poem The Masque of Anarchy he quoted on the back of *Sound Affects*.

At first, Weller assumed that Shelley was purely an English Romantic poet. It was his reading of Paul Foot's book *Red Shelley* that alerted him to the poet's radical politics, both personal and private. Shelley's work was therefore one of the elements that drew Paul towards socialism. Another major influence was the English author George Orwell, whose message of freedom and equality, especially in books such as *1984* and *Animal Farm*, struck a huge chord with Paul. Following Orwell were other works of note, especially Oscar Wilde's essay *The Soul of Man Under Socialism* and Robert Tressell's 1922 novel *The Ragged Trousered Philanthropists*. 'One of my favourite books of all time,' he said of the latter in 1985. 'I think books should be like records: they should entertain you but they should also give you something to think about.'

These works, coupled with his innate compassion for others, convinced Paul that socialism was the only way forward. He was at odds with the times. In 1979, the floundering Labour government had given way to the highly popular Conservative leader Margaret Thatcher. Labour's inability to control the unions and create a financial boom to allow them to push through left-wing policies had created an economy that favoured no one. A series of bust-and-boom monetary policies had enraged unions and capitalists alike, leading to the 'winter of discontent', a series of crippling strikes that paralysed the country. Thatcher's tough policies were busy creating even more division. The economy's emphasis had gradually shifted away from manufacture towards the financial markets. Tax was highly reduced for the rich. Class war in the 1980s centred on those who had and those who had not. A new breed of working-class entrepreneurs would emerge victorious from the money markets, while the traditional workers – the miners, the printers – would be put to death. All this pushed Paul further leftwards. He now saw the worker as the true hero of the times, not the film or pop star but the miner, the nurse, the builder, all those who worked long hours for low pay.

He made clear his thinking in this song. It was written at his small London flat to celebrate the men and the women 'who keep the country going', as Weller put it, receiving no congratulations for their heroic efforts in the public services. It is also Weller's attempt to redefine the word 'hero'. He notes people's tendency to regard pop stars as heroes, and vehemently disagrees with this assessment. 'Really,' he told *MM* in 1982, 'they are slobs, most of them, and parasites, and so are the politicians . . . it's the nurses and the miners and all those sort of people who are the real heroes . . . the main thing about this song, what I was intending, was to break down the myth about the "hero", all the pop stars and the rest who are regarded as such.' It is the album's only character-driven song, Paul recalling his own father coming home from the building site 'covered in shit and aches and pains', and then imagining him looking out the window and seeing enough tears to wash away the street, hearing also the sound of bells and watching a funeral march go by.

Until the 1990s, Paul felt twin impulses with regard to his talent: it was central to his being, it defined him, but it also singled him out from the crowd, and that was a consequence he was always keen to avoid. Socialism gave him a way to develop that talent and place it within a context that would be meaningful. He would see his talent as a contribution, on a par with that of a nurse, or a miner. 'I read a lot of things, people saying that I'm clever with words,' he told *MM*. 'But I don't really see it. Everyone is good at something, ain't they?'

Paul saw songwriting as his way of giving back to people. He wanted success so that he could do more to encourage others. He wanted his music to shake up the world, shake up lives, but he didn't want the trappings of pop stardom. Therefore, interviews were there to promote his music, not him. Records were to agitate as much as entertain, concerts were now celebrations, but also part rally. Various political organizations, Animal Rights and CND in particular, handed out leaflets to The Jam's legion of fans, who promptly screwed them up and chucked them away.

This wholesale embrace of socialism had some pleasing side effects: press interviews, for example, homed in on Paul's politics, to the exclusion of many other subjects. Reading these interviews now, it is striking how little is asked about Weller the man; there's so much on Weller the budding politico. No one (apart from *Melody Maker* in 1982) wants to know how or why songs are written; no one asks him about his lifestyle, his habits. Instead, there are endless discussions on the relationship between band and fans, how society should be organized, political theories, etc. It was a focus Weller could enjoy, if only because it deflected searching questions away from him.

It was in these discussions that Weller's political stance became crystal clear. He did not believe in the individual, but always in the collective. 'It's a constant argument I have with my old man,' he stated. 'He thinks that you do need political leaders, whereas I don't really. I believe you could do it by councils made up of working people. I think people, given the responsibility, can run their own lives, and I do believe in that.' Success was seen as important but only as a way of enabling others. Paul often talked of collaborations with young playwrights and poets. I clearly recall receiving a letter from him just prior to a 1981 CND benefit at the Embankment, asking me to ring him urgently as 'he had a great idea'. His idea was for me to write a piece of polemic prose and deliver it to the crowd. I DJ'd instead.

Paul was forever looking to ignite inspiration in others at this time. His belief was that everyone had potential. Unfortunately, the system killed that energy, and it therefore killed people. Paul's mission in life was to reverse that process, to stem the flow of the millions destined to become five o'clock heroes.

TWENTY-FOUR

Beat Surrender (Single, 1982)

Paul and Youth

In the summer of 1982, Paul decided to break up The Jam, start afresh. It was a decision so monumental that it reverberates to this day. Bass player Bruce Foxton and drummer Rick Buckler still haven't come to grips with it (as I write, they are currently performing under the name From The Jam), and Paul is still asked about his decision a quarter of a century after the event. Let me repeat that: Paul is still asked about his decision a quarter of a century after the event. It is hard to think of a parallel situation in contemporary music.

For many people, Weller's move was baffling. The Jam were the biggest band in the land, set to run for numerous years. Their creativity seemed undiminished, their status assured. By throwing it all aside, Paul was doing many things, not least challenging one of society's greatest beliefs: that success brings you happiness, that money, fame and widespread acclamation are the keys to the kingdom of eternal happiness. Breaking up The Jam put paid to that notion.

Weller's method of announcing the split was typical: he did it as a *coup de grâce*. Bruce and Rick were simply summoned to the Solid Bond Studios and told the dream was over. That was it. 'The trouble with Paul,' said Bruce afterwards, 'is that he never tells you what he is feeling.' There was no discussion – no point to it. Weller wanted out, and out he went.

In the rise to what The Beatles referred to as 'the toppermost of the poppermost', Weller had made another uneasy discovery about success: that a life of spontaneity is impossible to achieve. Even in the free and fab world of pop, routine was essential to maintain one's future. You might not be working nine to five, but there was always a schedule, one that consisted of album, tour, single, album, tour, tour, album, single, etc. It was an irritating fact of life that Weller had been keenly aware of for some years. This is him in 1979 talking to *Jamming* magazine: 'It just gets boring. It's all mapped out. You know that next year you have got two major British tours, an American tour, a European tour and an LP and two singles, the usual quota . . .' Paul used to love waking up full of vigour, not knowing what a day of promise would bring him. Now he knew exactly where he would be six months, two weeks and four days ahead.

What was the point of doing it if happiness and

contentment were not waiting for him at the end of it all? No point. Paul Weller was now twenty-four years old and, as he told the *NME*, he felt 'like a fucking machine'. The security of success did not entice him at all; in fact, it frightened him. So did the weight of the crowd's expectation upon his shoulders. Paul was Everyman, and the burden was killing him. Moreover, he was still obsessed with the subject of age. He firmly believed that pop belonged to the young, and at twenty-four he was already an old man. 'I wouldn't like,' he told the *NME* at the time, 'to be going out onstage singing When You're Young when I am thirty, doing Eton Rifles or Down In The Tube Station. I couldn't do it. I wouldn't be able to look people in the face.'

Other elements were also at work (see Shopping). Paul Weller's life was just too serious; there was no fun coursing through it. His was a world of crippling restriction. He was uptight, The Jam were uptight, everyone concerned was uptight. I remember going to Solid Bond Studios one evening to hear his song The Bitterest Pill (I Ever Had To Swallow). When I heard the line about autumn's breeze blowing leaves through his life, I laughed, as the writer had intended me to. 'You wanna watch yourself, son, you'll get a slap, you will,' said one of his minders, completely missing the joke. Paul just shuffled his feet, looked a little embarrassed. He couldn't win. He cracked jokes in public and no one knew whether to laugh or not. At the final Jam show (Brighton Conference Centre, 11 December 1982) he allowed his friend Pete Barrett and others to dress up and perform a pretentious dance routine for fun. The dancers were heckled and large coins were thrown at them.

That final gig was a nightmare of interruptions and sullen onstage behaviour. Paul Weller was at the prime of his life, rich and famous, and probably the unhappiest he had ever been. If you ask him when he was at his happiest in The Jam, he will tell you it was when the band were just about to break and they were all crammed into a van, driving up the motorway, shouting out their dreams of success to all who passed by.

In this song, Paul touches on all those themes. Lyrically it's a really good snapshot of where he was in his life at the time. He makes reference to his band with a biblical quote, making the point that wherever you go in life, to the top or the bottom, the bullshit is always there, it just appears under different titles. He comments on the dreams he now has and how his courage is such that it takes years to realize them; but no longer, for now he is stepping out from the shadows of sadness, brought out into sunlight by the sound of young, joyous bands making young, joyous music.

In Beat Surrender (he was considering the song A Solid Bond In Your Heart as the final Jam single but went – wisely – for this more uptempo and anthemic song), Paul joyfully celebrates the power of new bands playing new music. 'You'll hear me come running to sound of your strumming,' he sings and his championing of the young would remain a constant throughout his career. It was typical of him to finish

The Jam – a guitar band – with a song led by a deep rippling piano. He also gives a clue, in his lyrics about standing in the shadows for too long, to his new found determination to break out of his personal restrictions and see where he will end up as a person. It is a trait that would strongly develop over the next few years as the ghost of The Jam dogged his every move.

TWENTY-FIVE

Money Go Round (Single, 1983)

Paul and Finance

Ah, the filthy lucre, as Paul always referred to it. Another song title Ray Davies might just recognize was used as the basis for this bitter Style Council polemic against money's potential to create evil. Weller's writing here is inspired, extremely strong. One by one he targets the various sources of true power – Church, Government, Army – and, with words that are biting, satirical and funny, 'killing for peace, freedom and truth, but they're too old to go so they send the youth. Watch the money go round', he indicts their hypocrisy, their misuse of money – all set to a dirty funk workout. I remember Paul telling me that he had devised this single as a non-hit. He wanted a break from the charts, but he would have to wait for a few more years for that to happen. At this point, anything he touched, people bought in their masses.

Because of his success, Paul Weller has had serious money for several years now. At first, his attitude towards it was dismissive. There is a story that in 1977 the punk-conscious teenager wanted to give away his first advance from Polydor Records – some £6,000. His father would not have understood. I can imagine him looking at his son, absolute confusion on his face, gasping, 'You want to do *what*? You lost your fucking marbles?'

For John Weller, money was central to life (see Call Me). While you were on earth, you made as much as you could, when you could and where you could. His management of Paul had one basic aim: get rich. Where else would such an opportunity to line your pockets arise? The family had never been rich. That could now change, for ever. Their poverty as a family helps explain their drive to acquire riches. 'Money was always a bone of contention in our house,' Paul told *Uncut* in 2006. John's managerial strategy with cash was clear, and it never deviated: take as big an advance as possible from as many sources as possible. He often told me, 'Get the money up front – then they have to work to get it back.' John Weller, the champ boxer, waded into the music business throwing punches left, right and centre. He had no interest in the niceties of business, the fluffiness of false conversation, the illusion of friendship. Bollocks to all that. Just get the money. That was the only requirement.

In his days as manager, protecting son first, everyone

else second, John passed on his knowledge to Paul. With John having retired, Paul now looks after himself, with lawyers and the like to take care of contracts, details, etc. There is a feeling that, if anything, Paul has adopted an even harder approach than his father, that he is now obsessed with that ker-ching! moment when the till rings and the money pours in.

His songs English Rose, You're The Best Thing, Monday, That's Entertainment and Town Called Malice have been used to sell England as a holiday resort, Ribena, the National Lottery, Adidas and Clarks shoes respectively. (I can't help but think of a conversation at Paul's Holland Park dining table in 1988, when Paul asked everyone assembled if they thought he would ever give his songs to adverts. When it came to my turn, I said, 'No way whatsoever,' such was the importance of integrity to him. I had, of course, forgotten that two years earlier The Style Council had filmed an advert for Japanese TV at a time when revenues and record sales were low. The clue was right there.) Paul has also struck deals with clothing companies such as Fred Perry, Ben Sherman and Barracuta, as well as designed a range of shoes.

Indeed, the proliferation of Weller-related items in 2006 – singles, DVDs, concerts, merchandise, etc. – was at such a level that fans began seriously to question his motives. 'Is he the most re-issued artist at the moment?' wrote one fan on the Splinters' website. 'Cheeky bastards know full well that his audiences are loyal – in some cases too loyal. I'm jumping off the bandwagon. Single boxes, multi format releases (even for that shite *Catch: Flame* [the live album Paul issued in 2006]), laser discs, shoes, T-shirts, Fred Perry's, English Rose for holiday ads. Vote with your feet and your wallets! He'd be the first to moan if it was all done under the Small Faces name. I still think it's down to the bastards in suits somewhere advising him.' On a T-shirt designed by Paul that you could buy on the release of his last single Wild Blue Yonder, a fan wrote, 'The T-shirt is bloody awful. Did he really have a hand in designing it? It makes you wonder why Paul is putting his name to such shabby shite.' Another had this to say:

What I find to be more emotive is this fine line between loyalty and having the piss taken with a jumped up scheme that appears to have occupied Paul for all of 30 seconds (that includes signing the design notes that we can all try to win!). However, it does feel like someone, some-where is taking the piss! 'Yep!' chimed in our final contestant, 'together with flogging his back catalogue to death, exploiting his name, dodgy T-shirts and a stale set list etc etc, these are not the most fruitful times to follow him. Don't call me disloyal either!!!! I haven't even got my ticket for this tour, cos I know exactly what he'll do. I know I should get off my arse and be motivated. I guess I'm going totally against the grain but I can't help myself.'

It was not always thus. There was a different time, a different attitude. Steve Brookes makes note of Paul's current tight-fisted nature in his book *Keeping the*

Flame, but says that when they hung out together Paul was generous with his money, even if he didn't have much. As John Weller once told me, 'With Paul, say we get offered the number eight. The first thing I do is try to get ten, but it's a waste of time because Paul will only take two and that's it, end of discussion. I think he's mad, but what can I do?'

In his own financial matters, Paul operated a dual policy. If you hit a bad patch and went to him for help, he rarely, if ever, turned you down, and the transaction was always kept between you and him. He never brought it up in public, never embarrassed you. Furthermore, he never hassled you for its return. He knew about financial struggle, had grown up with it in front of his very eyes. He knew that if life had backed you up against the wall, it was odds on you would struggle to repay him. On the other hand, if he lent you money from his pocket – a tenner, a score, a nifty fifty – without fail, the first thing he would ask you the next time you met was, where's my money? His attitude was, whether he was a millionaire or not didn't matter. He should be treated the same.

When the mood took him, he could be extremely generous. Many times while walking among friends he has secretly pushed rolls of notes into my pocket, given me a little wink. In 1990 I left a staff job at the *NME*, went freelance. It was Christmas. Paul and I met for dinner. He asked if I was worried about cash, did I have work on the table. I said sure, told him how much I thought I would earn compared to what I had earned at the *NME*. He asked me how much that was. I told him. Two weeks later, on Christmas Day, he pushed an envelope towards me. Inside was a cheque for the exact amount I earned in a year as a staff writer at the *NME*.

Paul loved money. It satisfied his high sense of self-worth, allowed him the good things in life, the luxuries, the expensive designer clothes. Paul worked hard, worked well, so he was entitled to the best there was. He had deserved it. His socialism in the 1980s was not about taking people financially downwards, but upwards. He didn't want austerity, he wanted luxury. Yet he was careful with his money. As Anthony Storr observes about creative types, 'free spending is a form of letting go'.

But he was very careful not to appear flash – a working-class sin of great import. I remember when we struck the deal for the book *The Soul Stylists*. As it was his idea, I offered Paul part of my advance. 'Without being silly,' he shyly said, 'I don't really need the money. You have it.' A pause. 'But I want royalties and I want them up front.'

His desire not to be seen as flash extended to his property purchases. The house he now inhabits is one to gasp at. It really is a fantastic dwelling. Yet this is the first house of his like this. Most of the houses he bought over the years were never that individual or eye-catching. They were all in desirable West London residential areas, but were usually nondescript. It was classic Paul, caught in a trap: he had the money to spend but not the ego to do so overtly.

Paul played it low-key and, like his father, kept a tight ship financially. They rarely spent to accumulate, and that had an effect on Paul's art. Records, especially Style Council ones, often sound rushed and under-produced. Live concerts were everything but eye-catching in their design and lighting. (When we saw Paul live, a few of us would joke, 'Tour must be going well. He's added a light bulb to the stage . . .') Everything was kept to a minimum.

Money was also a marker for Paul. The more he made, the more his work was validated. Talking about Steve Marriott, Paul told me that for a songwriter, success is measured by the size of your cheque. It was absolutely flawed thinking. Nick Drake didn't make a penny in his lifetime. But for Paul, money was the best way for him to gauge his success. On that basis, he is still highly popular, still highly regarded, still spinning on that money go round.

TWENTY-SIX

Long Hot Summer (Single, 1983)

Paul, Nature and Bisexuality

During the Style Council years, the sun became a major symbol which Paul increasingly brought into his work. Many of his songs from this period carry references to the sun: Long Hot Summer, Spring Summer Autumn, A Summer Quartet, So Is The Sun . . .

Paul adores the sun. Winter is months of moaning about dark nights, cold air, biting rain. Summer is his time. The world becomes beautiful, inspirational; nature brings forth the luxury of warm air and light winds. Paul responds deeply to nature, to the changing seasons. He sees beauty in all of it, from a bare field with naked trees to the golden leaves of autumn. But it is that which is caressed by sunlight, be it a green field or an ocean wave, that speaks the strongest to him.

The bittersweet lyrics to this song, the way he

contrasts the beauty of summer with the loss of a loved one, aligned with a synthesizer riff that visually recalls ripples spreading languidly out across a river, made this single his most sensuous record to date, and it significantly increased his female following.

Despite his huge chart success with The Jam, Paul was not a major poster pin-up. The polemic nature of Jam records and their very male sound ensured that he was not viewed in a sexual light, although action was always available. He told *Sounds* in 1978 that after the first Jam tour he tired of 'the groupie scene'. Such hedonism would not have suited their very disciplined character anyway.

While in The Jam he did have adventures, but they were few and far between. He was also besotted with Gill for quite a few years.

Style Council songs such as Long Hot Summer changed all that. Walking around town with Paul at this time, it was striking the number of girls who now stopped him, fluttered eyelashes at him. Sometimes they went further. I remember Paul unexpectedly ringing me at my flat one night in the mid eighties, asking if I was free. I was surprised to hear from him because at the time he was madly in love with Dee C. Lee and spending most of his time with her.

I was free, and I met him in Bond Street, at about eight o'clock. As we walked towards a wine bar, he nonchalantly told me, 'We're celebrating tonight. Dee and I got engaged today.' Inside, a girl approached us at our table. She'd recognized Paul, had to tell him how much she loved his music. Above all, she loved the video for Long Hot Summer. 'I get that out when my flatmate is away,' she confided, 'and I am on my own, and I masturbate to it all night.'

Both of us sat there lost for words.

I once went out with a Jamaican soul girl, Stephanie. She was a clubber; The Jam and rock culture had barely touched her life. I took her round to Paul's house one night. Somehow, The Jam came up in conversation.

From out of nowhere, she said to Paul, 'So, are you still in the National Front?'

'What?' Paul replied.

'What?' said everyone else present.

'Oh, I'm sorry,' she said. 'It's just that I used to see you on TV with a short haircut being really angry so I thought you were sort of like a skinhead or something.'

This was the image a lot of women had of Paul.

His wife, Dee C. Lee, for example. When she worked her first Style Council session at the Solid Bond Studios, Paul found her in the corridor looking at the gold discs he had accumulated with The Jam on the wall.

'Who's this Jam group then?' Dee asked him in all innocence.

'Oh, some crap group,' Paul replied.

When Paul began The Style Council, women began to take notice. Through languid records such as Long Hot Summer, Paul found a new audience. He also discovered that one surefire way to put as much distance between himself and his Jam audience was to start exploiting sex.

One important model was the playwright Joe Orton, who had been murdered in August 1967 by his lover, Kenneth Halliwell. Orton's tough persona, wit and daring use of gay themes in his work, and this at a time when homosexuality was illegal, excited Paul. Orton's gayness was very masculine: he was highly promiscuous, and he used his talents to challenge the very people Paul had attacked in Jam songs.

Paul read John Lahr's excellent Orton biography *Prick Up Your Ears* and assimilated aspects of Orton's character and attitude into his own work. He wrote a song called Up For Grabs!, a play on the title Orton had used for his unfilmed script for The Beatles, and worked on a song with the singer Tracie which he called The Boy Hairdresser, named after Orton's posthumously published novel. He took things further with the video for this song, which in part featured shots of Paul and his musical partner Mick Talbot lying by a river, tickling each other's ears. Paul is dressed only in cut-off jeans, his skin oiled. Polydor Records panicked when they saw it, said it had to be reshot. In response, Paul sent the head of the company a video with a note saying, 'We have re-shot the video, here it is.' The video he sent was pornographic.

'It is often affirmed,' Anthony Storr states, 'that creativity is an expression of the bisexuality which can be discerned within most human beings.' In The Style Council, Paul allowed that part of his character to flourish, although he never, as far as I know, acted on any gay impulses. He once told an interviewer, casually, that the singer Marilyn had offered him oral sex. 'I was mildly interested,' he said, 'but when it came to it, I didn't fancy it.' Certainly he cast appreciative eyes over well-dressed good-looking fellas, but his admiration tended to be more aesthetic than sexual. After all, Paul is a great dresser himself and such men always have a feminine side, as his use of pastel colours shows us. Gays certainly liked Paul, saw something in him they felt was simpatico, but although he liked their company and liked to flirt with them, he never crossed the line.

Throughout the 1980s, certainly in his attempts to wind up his Jam audience, Paul gleefully used gay imagery. Press releases of him and Mick applying make-up were released, the Long Hot Summer video was made, and Paul accepted a photo session with Boy George, the pair of them smiling away at each other. This was a world away from The Jam, both musically and image-wise. It can be argued that the Council's first two singles, Speak Like A Child and Money Go Round, could have fitted somewhere within the later Jam canon. But Long Hot Summer never could.

Paul was now fiercely anti rock music. It was a sham, he claimed, a charade. Soulful expression was the only thing that mattered (indeed, the riff to Long Hot Summer was inspired by the work of a British eighties soul band called Imagination). Paul also became extremely playful. Press releases were sent out which spoke of walking on water in France, or playing flugel-horns in the Swiss Alps. Adverts appeared in a thousand different languages. A character called The

Paul in Japan in 1982, the year
he would break up The Jam.

Left: The author with Paul as he goes through his fan mail.

Left: The author with Paul and Pete Townshend, April 1980. The meeting was not successful, although the two musicians would later develop a much better relationship.

Below: The Jam in the suits 'inspired' by Dr Feelgood guitarist, Wilko Johnson.

Right: The band always disliked the other sides of their job, such as looking happy in pictures.

Background: Paul with his father, John. This unique father-and-son relationship took a working-class family from Woking to national recognition.

Below left: In most Jam photographs Paul's sense of style allowed him to stand out. This is no exception.

Below right: Keeping lines of communication open with the fans was always a big part of The Jam's operations.

Right: Paul helping Bob Geldof the day before the recording of the Band Aid song, 'Do They Know It's Christmas?' Paul's participation in this song has always been vastly underplayed.

Left: Paul with Jimmy Somerville of Bronski Beat, Ken Livingstone, Neil Kinnock and Billy Bragg at the launch of the Red Wedge movement. Paul's involvement would put him off party politics for good.

Left: The author with The Style Council, who were in Paris to shoot the cover for the *Café Bleu* album in 1984.

Left: A famous shot of Paul illustrating the difference between his idea of Mod and that of his then audience.

Right: Portrait of the young man as a budding playboy.

Paul looking Wilde and moody, sporting the haircut that caused those close to him to give him the nickname Herr Weller.

Left: Paul with Mick Talbot, a man of consummate skill and taste.

Left: Paul, the author, and friend Johnny Chandler in Paul's back garden, *c.* 1990. Neither of them is close to Paul now.

Below: Paul leaving the stage of the Royal Albert Hall having just performed with Ronnie Wood at the 2004 benefit concert for Ronnie Lane.

Below left: Paul with Noel Gallagher of Oasis, a friendship based on Beatles, humour and understanding.

Below right: Paul with one of his all-time heroes, Ray Davies of The Kinks. It was his music that inspired Paul to write the Jam breakthrough album, *All Mod Cons*.

Paul at Glastonbury in 2007, trying to recapture his amazing performance of 1994 at the same venue.

Right: Paul with his partner Sammi at the dinner for sleeve designer Simon Halfon's fortieth birthday. Paul and Sammi have two children together.

Paul with stubble, grappling with time.

Cappuccino Kid was invented, and his writings, pretentious and vivid, biting and funny, appeared on every Style Council sleeve. Videos were shot with Paul dancing in a pinstripe suit, his hair slicked back, and a million Mods cried, you've broken one of the Ten Commandments by using grease in your hair! He was filmed on top of a bus dancing towards the camera, clicking his fingers, swaying his hips, laughing, and a million girls suddenly asked, who is this?

Long Hot Summer was a new musical direction for Paul. It told us that he had now stopped struggling against the world, and begun to see it in all its brilliant colours.

TWENTY-SEVEN

Headstart For Happiness
(*Café Bleu*, 1984)

Paul and Clichés

With his song Ghosts, Paul hit upon a new lyrical approach, one that homed in on the personal and forsook the social and the political. He continued to develop this approach in The Style Council, in songs such as Strength Of Your Nature, and in the second version of this song, Headstart, in which his added words extol the value of thinking positively (and in doing so reveal a crucial aspect of his continued success).

There are two versions of this song: the original acoustic version, which appeared as the B side to Money Go Round, and this version, made with a full band. (It is interesting to note how many times Paul revisited his songs during this period, a musical trait which disappeared, on record at least, from the mid

1980s onwards.) In the new version, Paul added verses that seek to inspire people, to tell each and every one that inside them is the potential to realize their dreams. All you need is confidence.

Weller was unique among our little gang in that way: although besieged with doubt on many occasions, he was always far more confident and sure of himself than his friends. The way he dressed, the assured way in which he carried himself, his little mannerisms, all this reflected a confidence that was always there to be called upon in times of crisis. Sometimes, the confidence turned to arrogance. Here he is as a young buck in 1977, talking about meeting John Entwistle of The Who for the first time: 'I thought him really ordinary and boring so I gave him my autograph and went home . . .'

On the other hand, Paul recognized what a vital asset he had been blessed with, and he generously tried to spread it to others. One thinks here of his quote to *Smash Hits*, that he is not special because he is Paul Weller from The Jam and has had number one hit records, he is special because he is human and therefore 'anyone can potentially feel this way'. Or one recalls the way he was forever trying to encourage people he thought had promise; two admirable traits which seemed to have dimmed with the years. One of Paul's great needs at this stage in his career was to break the myth of the pop star, to demystify the process so that the pop star is no different to, say, the hairdresser – the establishment of a level playing field, in other words, a position all socialists seek. (He would persist with this notion in later years, but from a selfish point of view, not a political one. See Everything Has A Price To Pay.)

Although most of his contemporaries in the song-writing field are affected by shyness, it is vital that the musician who seeks to stay the course has a great sense of belief in himself, otherwise he is dead meat. Paul's parents may have mollycoddled him, but their love also gave him that great quality and allowed him to step up – and, just as important, keep stepping up, year after year. If you don't believe in yourself, how can you persuade anyone else to? Even if Paul doubted much of what he said, he still said it so as to maintain his persona, the persona that would become an obsession for some fans and a source of inspiration for others. Without that confidence, or patina of confidence, people in the street wouldn't have referred to him as the King of England. People respond to strength in others they admire, if not like. Paul goes his own way, never letting record companies or indeed his audience dictate his next move. At times, that takes balls.

Headstart's dramatic middle eight was lifted whole-sale from The Young Rascals' song A Girl Like You, but that doesn't matter as such. Weller was confident enough to create from this a song that has lasted the years, given hope to many, and even inspiration to a few.

TWENTY-EIGHT

It Just Came To Pieces (In My Hands)
(B Side of Solid Bond In Your Heart,
1984)

Paul and Fame (Part Three)

This was the first of Paul's songs to try to demystify his role as a star, to publicly confess to a personal and very real fallibility. He wanted to make the public figure human, to point out his many weaknesses, to say once again that success is an illusion. His motives for doing so were both selfish and honourable.

For Paul, the worship of the star was a flawed process. It created a mirage which disallowed meaningful and truthful communication. When people saw Paul, they gasped. They already had an impression of him set hard in their minds. True communication was not possible in such circumstances. 'I hate using these clichés like "success", "fame", "sex" and "drugs",' he wrote in the Lawrence Watson photographic record of him *Days Lose Their Names and Time Slips Away*, 'because they are myths created to hold the masses in suspension and out of the truth. It's the middle-class revolution, creating its own spells to sell to the working class . . .' By attacking such thinking, Paul was hoping to alleviate some of the burden of being a public figure. As we know, he hated being singled out in the crowd, being looked at, being talked about as he passed by. It unnerved him. I remember going to the Tate Britain with him and a guard there staring at him the whole time, Paul's anger rising by the second at this blatant intrusion.

And Paul being Paul, the first person he was going to examine and find wanting was, of course, himself. I recall meeting him at Frank's café in Neal St, Covent Garden, one Saturday afternoon in the early eighties, and him looking glum, distracted.

'What's up?' I asked.

'It's my ego,' he replied. 'I've got to fight it, stop it running away with itself.'

Then he retreated back into his shell, and left shortly afterwards. It was an experience few of us can imagine having.

This song is about ego deflation, about toppling pretensions, and ironically it was this kind of brutal honesty that won Paul even more favour with his audience and increased his 'success'. Paul wanted respect and recognition for his work, not for his character. That was one of the reasons why he refused to play the game and become as well known as a Rod Stewart or a Liam Gallagher. He knew well that he was not built to withstand the intensity of the public gaze, that it would lead him away from that which was of the utmost importance to him, writing songs. Without that outlet, he would literally crumble into a thousand different pieces. This song, made attractive by the use of repeated a cappella vocal lines and compelling word-play, was a reminder to himself of that frightening possibility.

TWENTY-NINE

Ghosts Of Dachau (B Side of Shout To The Top, 1984)

Paul and Clichés

Evidence, certainly, of Paul's increasing maturity as a lyricist. Paul visited Dachau while on tour in Germany and was struck by the fact that no birds go near the place. I also recall lending him a book on the concentration camps called *Ashes and Diamonds*, although in one of our last conversations he said it was another book on the same subject that pushed him into writing this sad lament.

The finished article could have been mawkish, but by making the focus of the song a love story featuring two prisoners, Paul circumvents the problem. He writes about beauty in scabs, the loss of memory in the space we call dark. It is extremely moving, and musically very haunting. Not for the first time, Paul's vocal is reminiscent of David Bowie's early London voice – a charge I am sure he would dismiss, but one that remains true simply through geography: Bowie and Weller grew up not that far from each other and listened to several of the same artists.

THIRTY

The Piccadilly Trail (B Side of Shout To The Top, 1984)

Paul and Recording

Paul once told me that this song concerned a gay relationship gone wrong, the story of a teacher (or some such person) who comes to London, drops into Soho and falls for a rent boy. But on their next date the boy fails to show and is nowhere to be found, so our forlorn hero wanders the 10p arcades amid the poison gossip, now so scared of the weeks ahead. It is a beautiful song with a great languid riff running throughout, one in keeping with Paul's philosophy of providing great B sides to singles.

Often these songs were not given as much attention in the studio as the A sides and therefore seemed to breathe better than their counterparts. The number of hours I spent in Solid Bond Studios listening to bass guitars being equalized, guitars being tweaked and drums being balanced I cannot tell you, all the time thinking that no one was going to take this record back to their local shop and demand a refund because the bass hadn't been equalized enough or the tweaking and the balancing weren't quite up to scratch. It also amazed me how comfortable Paul, this bag of nerves, this constant mover, was to spend hour after hour after hour after hour with producers and engineers, recording and honing and God knows what else. I would have thought this the worst part of his job, but he seemed to thrive on it. It allowed him to watch his art take shape.

As the years went by his recording habits changed. For The Jam and The Style Council, it was generally a case of recording by day: clocking in during the morning, taking off early evening, the time filled with tea and coffee, a trip to the café, and cigarettes, countless cigarettes. In his solo career, that changed. Night-time became the right time, a space filled with booze and other accoutrements, and, of course, cigarettes, countless cigarettes.

And, unfortunately, not writing or recording any more love songs with this kind of subject matter, as his music is now so very masculine.

THIRTY-ONE

You're The Best Thing (Single, 1984)

Paul and Romance

One Saturday afternoon I was sat in a West End café with Paul when this song came on the radio. Paul cocked an ear, listened for a bit, turned to me and said, 'You know, I can't believe I wrote this song. I can't believe I came up with that riff.' Anthony Storr, again: 'There are many people who underestimate their strength, forcefulness and power to act, because they think of themselves as passive vessels waiting to be filled.'

The early eighties was a prolific time for Paul. Between 1980 and 1982 he released thirty-six Jam songs, fourteen of which I would nominate as enduring (Dreams Of Children, Start!, Liza Radley, Pretty Green, Monday, That's Entertainment, Dream Time, Man In The Corner Shop, Tales From The Riverbank, Town

Called Malice, Shopping, Beat Surrender, Ghosts, Carnation). Over the next two years he released thirty-two Style Council songs, thirteen of which I think have stood the test of time (Speak Like A Child, Money Go Round, Long Hot Summer, It Just Came To Pieces, The Paris Match, Spring Summer Autumn, Ghosts Of Dachau, The Piccadilly Trail, Headstart For Happiness, Here's One That Got Away, Shout To The Top, The Whole Point Of No Return, My Ever Changing Moods).

The musical side he developed best with The Style Council was his balladeering. A sensitive side rarely seen in The Jam emerged. Check out the opening lyrics of this song about how he eschews power-crazy ways and doesn't want riches, how love is all he needs. (Today, he follows the path that leads away from such high moral notions. You can hear this in his songs used on TV adverts, a position that the Weller of the eighties would never have accepted.) Songs such as this, Paris Match, Spring Summer Autumn, Ghosts Of Dachau and The Piccadilly Trail show a depth and sensitivity that was never so evident in Jam compositions. Although he might have alienated a few Jam fans with this new musical direction, his carefree persona and his constant wind-ups, the audience he picked up through beautiful love songs such as this more than compensated. In fact, I was once told that record-wise, The Style Council actually outsold The Jam. Certainly Paul's standing as a songwriter was immeasurably strengthened by his Style Council work, his decision to split The Jam brilliantly vindicated by the supple beauty of much of his work.

You're The Best Thing was a huge hit for Paul and one that certainly strengthened and increased his female fan base. It showed an innate understanding of the craft of mainstream songwriting, just as did his later hit, You Do Something To Me. Why, even Tony Blackburn would have doffed his hairpiece to this song.

THIRTY-TWO

Walls Come Tumbling Down
(Single, 1984)

Paul and Other Bands

The second line of this song, Weller's assertion that you do *not* have to relax, was a direct dig at the band Frankie Goes To Hollywood. Their single, Relax, had recently hit the number one spot. The band's decadent image riled Paul.

Internationally, Ronald Reagan's USA lurched ever closer to nuclear confrontation with Russia. At home, Thatcherism was at its height, and every day it felt as if the working class were being attacked from all sides. ('No peace for the wicked', Paul sang on the 1985 song The Lodgers, 'only war on the poor'.) Unemployment figures were staggeringly high, the printers were about to strike, the miners were soon to follow. A tone of high amorality made itself distinct in society, the notion that getting rich at any cost was acceptable. At the same time, documentaries showing families scavenging on rubbish tips became a regular item on television. Thatcher's statement on the day of her election victory in 1979, that she would bring harmony where there was division, was perhaps the greatest piece of disinformation ever issued from Number Ten. Instead, it felt as if Thatcher had launched a revenge mission on anyone who had ever harmed her party. The result was that post-war Britain had never felt so divided.

For a band such as Frankie to be cavorting around in leather chaps making suggestive remarks was, for the highly politicized Weller, the height of irresponsibility. He still saw music as a vital instrument of change, a weapon to be used against the forces of darkness. Bands such as Frankie, with their orgiastic celebrations of sexuality, aligned with the growing influence of London's apolitical club scene, made Paul liken the situation to the last days of Rome: Britain on its knees, and everyone drunk and in orgies (a situation, incidentally, with which I am sure today he would join in most enthusiastically).

Paul Weller's anger and intolerance at bands failing to follow his way was nothing new. From day one he has been coating off bands, and he has never stopped. In fact, such has been the regularity of his vitriol towards others that in 1995 a *Mojo* writer, Mat Snow, was moved to tell him, 'Since you first appeared it seems to have been you versus everyone else.'

'I've always been like that,' Weller candidly admitted. 'It's my own arrogance.'

In his first *NME* interview, in April 1977, he proclaimed, 'You can't play rock'n'roll when you've got a beer gut.' He then stated that Pete Townshend's songs had of late been 'so self indulgent'. Paul McCartney was kind of OK, but 'Lennon is the only one who hasn't sold out'. And so the tone was set. This is the clean-living Paul in a later *NME* interview: 'You know all these rock casualties? They fucking deserve it. I don't give a shit about them. They don't deserve to be written about or felt sorry for, or anything. It's tough shit.'

Reading his biting criticism of others, and being exposed to it in conversations, I would surmise that it was hypocrisy, bad image, meaningless music and an inability to play one's instrument properly – a four-pronged beast – that were guaranteed to set him on fire. The 1980s, therefore, saw him spitting even more bullets than usual. In that decade, the growing influence of technology in studios took pop away from its organic sound. Drum machines and synthesizers replaced humans and allowed those of very limited ability the chance to enter the pop world. Never before had so many bad singers stood before so many microphones.

This perceived downturn in standards was something that irked Weller immensely. He was, after all, a man who had spent years in bars and pubs, bedrooms and sitting rooms, assiduously learning his craft. Once, on a flight back from the San Remo Festival which also carried various members of Duran Duran, Spandau Ballet and Depeche Mode, he lambasted their arrogance, the way they carried themselves as if they were really special. 'None of them,' he raged, 'could sing or play or write a decent fucking tune.' He once revealed his idea to me that he wanted to organize a festival in France, with the cream of this crop head-lining. He would charter a plane to take these bands to the site, but halfway over the Channel shoot it down. 'If Maggie Thatcher,' he once said, 'was in a band, she would be in Duran Duran.'

Such comments hardly endeared him to this new generation of musicians. In 1984, Bob Geldof – whom Weller had, of course, criticized several times – contacted Paul. He wanted his help to write and prepare a song that would feature every major artist and raise money to fight starvation in Africa. The project would be called Band Aid. Paul agreed to help, working with Geldof on the song itself on the Saturday, and then turning up the next day for the all-star recording. Film of the stars arriving for the day's recording brilliantly illustrates the gulf between Weller and his eighties contemporaries. Limo after limo pulls up and disgorges smiling pop stars into the studio. Paul arrives by strolling down the street with his slicked-back hair and walking cane, looking like he has just got off the number ten bus. Which I think he had. At the session itself, he found himself ostracized, studiously ignored by many. When interviewed in the studio, he said, 'I'm hardly everybody's favourite person. They just seem to ignore me. I don't blame them. The cause is the only common thing between us, otherwise you'd never have gotten all these bands together – especially with me here.'

Understandably, Paul did not hang out with any musicians until the mid 1990s. Not one. They all fell drastically short of his standards. Either they were Thatcherite wankers or they should know better. 'David Bowie and Macca still doing *Top of the Pops* at fifty?' he once exclaimed. 'You're fucking joking, mate. It's depressing. I will not do that, mate.'

Weller's inability to live and let live has been a constant. When *Mojo* magazine featured Paul in an article alongside Duran Duran and George Michael, he was absolutely furious. He told the writer in his next *Mojo* interview, 'To be put with them I take as a personal insult.' And here is Paul in 2006 on previous winners of the Brits Lifetime Award.

Bob Geldof? 'Can't be for his music, man. I mean, if it's for his charity work in Africa, then you can't knock it. But The Boomtown Rats? Fuck off.'

Tom Jones? 'Tom's cool, man. I'd sooner see Tom win it than Bob fucking Geldof. Or should I say Sir Bob.'

Sting and The Police? 'Fucking horrible . . . wankers.'

U2? 'Pseudo American rubbish.'

Fleetwood Mac? 'I've got Albatross on my jukebox, but that was a different fucking band. I ain't having *Tusk* and all that bollocks.'

The Bee Gees? 'Good songwriters, but grown men on helium. It's not good.'

Bowie? 'No. Wrong! I like about three records of his: Low, Hunky Dory and Can't Help Thinking About Me. The rest is pish!'

Van Morrison? 'Top boy.'

Rod Stewart? 'Never been a fan.'

Freddie Mercury? 'Said he wanted to bring ballet to the working classes. What a cunt!'

Status Quo he had a lot of time for; Eric Clapton, not really, much prefer the originals.

Weller lashed out at most people, and sometimes with extremely comic results. After lunch one day, Simon Halfon gave Paul and me a lift in his 1967 Mustang. I was sat in the back, Paul and Simon up front. Simon, who was driving, turned on the car radio.

'Turn that fucking shit off,' Paul snapped after about twenty seconds.

'For God's sake,' Simon shouted back, 'it's you, you idiot.'

And it was. It was The Changing Man by Paul Weller blaring through.

Once, at a gig in Dublin, I introduced Paul to the U2 guitarist The Edge. They were forced to shake hands, and Paul has never forgiven me for it.

Funny stuff, but it is incorrect to paint Paul as a bitter man coating off every band in existence, even if he does it to himself as well. In truth, Paul has championed many bands. Either he has written for them, taken them on tour, enthused about them in the press, or raved about them to influential people. He wrote a song called Dr Love for Bananarama, another one called Waiting On The Connection for a London funk band called Push. He has appeared on several artists' records, including Peter Gabriel, Mother Earth, Ocean Colour

Scene, The Beautiful South, Robert Wyatt, Dr John, Oasis, Carleen Anderson and Dr Robert (see also English Rose). The last-named told me how generous in spirit he felt Paul had been at the session he came to, making all kinds of suggestions and offers that Robert found useful and staying until everything was completed. Perhaps Paul was making up for his behaviour during the recording sessions for Slam Slam, the solo project of Paul's then wife, Dee C. Lee.

Dee had asked Dr Robert to produce the album. Robert agreed, and they began recording in 1988 at Solid Bond Studios. Paul showed up to all the sessions, and every ten minutes or so offered advice. Robert would take so much until finally he would have to remind Paul that he was the producer, that he made the decisions. Paul would back down straight away, agreeing with Robert's position. Of course he was the producer, Paul would admit, it was his call. Pacified, Robert would resume work. Ten minutes later, Paul would start up again with the suggestions.

The singer Carleen Anderson, formerly of the Young Disciples, worked closely with Paul on her album *Blessed Burden*. Paul co-wrote two songs with her, Burning Bridges and I'm Gonna Miss You, produced another six, and played a variety of instruments. (No doubt he saw Carleen Anderson as his PP Arnold, the American singer Weller's hero Steve Marriott helped write and produce for back in the sixties.) Carleen returned the favour by contributing celestial vocals to Wings Of Speed, one of Paul's strongest ever ballads, and the song that ends his million-selling album *Stanley Road*.

It was during the making of that album that Paul invited Steve Winwood, a musician he much admired, to play on two songs, Pink On White Walls and The Woodcutter's Son. Winwood's professionalism and his egoless demeanour impressed Paul, although, according to one source present at the time, Paul was jittery the whole time Winwood was there.

Paul has now met all his heroes, apart from Steve Marriott whom he refused to see when I spoke to the man for the *NME* in 1984. He simply didn't want his illusions shattered. His childhood hero, Paul McCartney, he first met at Air Studios in 1982 when he was making *The Gift*. The resulting photo was memorable not for the fact that the two Pauls are together, but for the way in which Weller's Dennis the Menace badge draws your attention. Over a decade later, at Abbey Road Studios in London on 4 September 1995, he worked with McCartney, recording a version of the Beatles song Come Together for an album designed to raise money for children living in war zones.

McCartney arrived at about two in the afternoon to find a studio filled with names such as Noel Gallagher, Carleen Anderson (who actually curtsied when she met Macca), Steve Cradock, Damon Minchella, Marco Nelson, Andy MacDonald (head of Independiente Records, Paul's label), Johnny Depp and Kate Moss. Stella McCartney also attended. (Macca once expressed his relief that Paul never married Stella. He couldn't have handled a Stella Weller in the family.) The session was highly memorable, McCartney, in particular, affable and approachable. At one point, as he stood talking to Paul, I pointed out to him that thirty-three years ago to the actual day, in that very studio, he had been cutting The Beatles' debut single Love Me Do.

'My God,' McCartney said. 'I remember that session so well. We were really out to beat Gerry and the Pacemakers. That was what we had to do that day, beat Gerry and the Pacemakers. Later on it was the Dave Clark Five, got to beat the Dave Clark Five.'

Weller, in a tone dryer than the desert, said, 'Um, think you might have done it, mate.'

The recording booth at Abbey Road Studios is reached from the ground floor by some stairs. Standing in that studio during the session, looking down, was Paul Weller, guiding Paul McCartney, who was sat down on the floor playing his guitar. When the session finished, Paul sat outside the studios in the cold night air, waiting for a cab. He turned to me and said, 'That's it now, done it all.'

The Who's Pete Townshend was another early obsession of his. When Paul first came to prominence, the *NME* writers Tony Parsons and Julie Burchill thought it would be a great idea to drive him down to Twickenham to meet Townshend. Unfortunately, Townshend was not at home, but I thought it such a great idea that I nicked it when I was at *Melody Maker*. In early April 1980 the two finally met, at The Who's Trinifold offices on London's famous Wardour Street.

They had nothing in common. Townshend was now

middle-aged and into drink; Weller was twenty-two and absolutely committed to his vision of music as a force for change, to steering as far away as possible from anything that reeked of rock stardom cliché. The two did not connect at all. Weller was diplomatic about a Who show he had seen at the Rainbow, Townshend kept on about how it was important not to ignore America – a position Paul disagreed with straight away. The end moved into sight when Paul asked Townshend how he decided on what recording studio to use, and Townshend replied, 'By the girl at the reception desk and whether you want to fuck her or not.' Perhaps it was this occasion that convinced Paul never to meet his idols.

Later, Townshend wrote a piece for *Time Out* magazine on Paul. In it, he called Paul 'a Hero, a British Hero'. He considered how Paul's fans identified with Jam music, noting, 'There is no bitterness in Weller's writing that isn't fully shared by his fans. Everything that is wrong with the world is someone else's fault. God is not in his heaven, and if he is then he isn't doing a very good job of handling the population explosion, political corruption and global disintegration.' He added,

'I read recently that Paul Weller has given up night-clubs, booze and drugs, and I suppose they do all go hand in hand. He is quite clearly a man of principle, but isn't he rejecting the only group of people who can really understand his frustrations? Has a musician ever changed any part of the world? Weller seems willing to deal only with

Britain at this stage; he leaves America to the Americans and is apparently so disdainful of the States that it causes him pain to even talk about the place.'

He also made a telling point about image and stardom – and having lived with the implications of both since 1965, one presumes that Townshend has some knowledge of the subject matter.

Weller quite consciously tries to represent a kind of Being that manages to be aloof and proud in the middle of ennui. He is also very aware that he is under a microscope. I have never come across any other artist or writer so afraid of appearing hypocritical; he is genuinely concerned that anyone who identifies with his feelings should not be let down. He has no large expensive car, shuns large houses and, I suspect, attempts to use his money wisely (if he knows how to do it I wish he'd write a song about it – it would do us all a world of good). But he is a Star. He himself carefully engineers what kind of Star and in what kind of stratosphere he shines; never too grand, never too remote.

When he was asked about this piece by the *NME* in 1982, Weller curtly replied, 'Didn't really understand it, and the bits I did were a load of old bollocks.'

In 1989, while rehearsing at Nomis Studios for his Acid House-influenced show at the Royal Albert Hall (one of his bravest ever shows), Paul discovered that The Who had been booked into the adjacent studio, rehearsing for a comeback tour of the States. Chatting to one of the band's roadies one day, Weller asked why the band were re-forming, especially as Townshend had to play within a glass frame so as to protect his hearing.

'John Entwistle is broke,' the roadie said. 'He's down to his last four million.'

That then became a running joke between Paul and me.

'I see so-and-so is back on the road.'

'Yeah, poor sod, must be down to his last four million.'

Paul once did some work at Entwistle's home recording studio, part of the huge mansion he lived in, complete with a bar. Paul's comment on this lifestyle? 'It's nice to see how seventies rock stars used to live.' There was more short shrift when Paul asked Townshend why The Who were playing America.

'To re-educate the American kids with r'n'b music,' Townshend replied.

'You're fucking joking, aren't you?' Paul blurted out.

End of conversation.

These days, Pete Townshend and Paul Weller are far more simpatico, and that's because time changes characters: Townshend is now clean and sober, while the Paul Weller of today is a million miles away from the Paul Weller of The Jam or The Style Council. When he saw The Who at the Royal Albert Hall two years ago, Weller did not sneer and pronounce the band crap, as he would have done twenty years ago. Instead, he was totally enthused. He told me that Townshend's guitar playing had made him feel like a kid again, that the man's power and dynamics and showmanship made him want to go home, get his guitar out and play.

He has, in fact, played with Townshend. Three years ago, they duetted at a charity show at the Royal Albert Hall, covering the Townshend song So Sad About Us on acoustic guitars. Weller had suggested they do Sunrise, one of his favourite songs from the *Who Sell Out* album, but Pete couldn't recall the chords and neither could work them out anyway.

Paul has also connected with Ray Davies of The Kinks. In 1986 he offered him a composition called (I think) My Very Good Friend, but was turned down. He did see him in concert at the Festival Hall on London's South Bank about two years ago, though.

'Brilliant,' he told me, 'every song was a gem.'

'Did you meet him?' I asked.

'Yeah. You know me, got pissed, went backstage and kept telling him how much I loved him. He was just standing there going, "Yeah, OK." ' (Another running joke between us: guys who get drunk or high and then slobber over each other crying, 'I love you. No, I do, I love you.')

As I said, Paul never met Steve Marriott or Ronnie Lane from The Small Faces. He did, however, meet and work on separate occasions with their drummer, Kenney Jones (whose 1960s Mini Paul used as a template for his Mini), and organist Ian McLagan.

I took Paul to a preview of a documentary about The Action once, and he came away with the autographs of those band members present. He met Roy Wood at

Aston Villa Leisure Centre and chewed his ear off about obscure Move B sides, and songs such as Beautiful Daughter, which Paul especially loves. (Lovers of Paul's song Misty Morning, incidentally, might be intrigued to learn of a Move LP song called Mist On A Monday Morning.) He also worked with people such as Robert Kirby, the man who did the string arrangements for the late Nick Drake, another musician Paul admired. In the early nineties he met the ex-Rolling Stones producer Jimmy Miller with a view to working with him, but Miller, who had not long to live, turned Paul down. He did offer him one bit of advice, though, telling him to watch his tendency to rush the words when he sang. Paul also sent demos to the legendary producer Glyn Johns (Stones, Beatles, Small Faces, to name but three fair to middling acts he worked with), but Johns too refused the gig, saying he had nothing to bring to the table. When they did finally meet to work on a Small Faces tribute album, Paul couldn't help having a little dig at him by mentioning the incident.

The musician Paul has perhaps got closer to than any-one else is Oasis's Noel Gallagher. They first met at the Glastonbury Festival in 1994, when Paul usurped the headliner Elvis Costello by turning in a set that was breathtaking in its scope and energy. Afterwards we went for a drink in the artists tent and bumped into Noel, who was on the way out. Paul told him he had seen the band's video for Supersonic and enjoyed both song and film. Noel smiled shyly, said thanks, then quickly moved off. Later, when Noel was living at the

Smiths guitarist Johnny Marr's flat in Fulham, he invited both me and Paul round. There were drinks, there were rare Beatles tapes, there was a sense of working-class kinship forged in council estate life.

Most of the time, Noel Gallagher is a highly personable and warm human being. He is also a huge Weller fan. As he got to know Paul, he too saw the man's many sides, often making fun of them. 'He is Victor Meldrew with a suntan,' he once said of Paul's constant moaning. He also caught Paul out a few times. At a Sheffield Arena gig, Noel debuted his classic song Don't Look Back In Anger on acoustic guitar. Afterwards, he asked Paul what he thought of the new song. Fucking great, Paul replied. It was only when they looked at the hidden CCTV footage taken in their dressing room (installed to catch some of the many thieves who were circling the band) that they saw Paul enter the room and take a drink while Noel played out the song in the arena.

Inevitably, Paul and Noel began to play together, making guest appearances on records and at gigs. Paul has played with Oasis on stage in London, Noel with Paul at festivals. Paul covered the Oasis song One Way Street, while on one Paul Weller tour Noel was the surprise support act.

The two of them have shared many nights and days filled with drink and arguments and laughs and revelations. But they differ in significant ways. For a start, Noel is in no way as driven as Paul. If he can get away with watching TV all day, he will. For Paul, such laziness is an anathema, simply wrong. You should work as much as you can whenever you can. Noel thoroughly enjoys the rock star life, the attention, the massive gigs, the press. Paul, as we know, dismisses this lifestyle. Then there's their musical tastes: Noel's are far more rock-orientated – Pistols, Bowie, Iggy Pop; Paul's veer more into r'n'b and jazz. Yet they have a deep affection for each other. Noel might bristle at some of Paul's snipings, and Paul might question Noel's tendency to tell larger-than-life stories, but there is a genuine respect and love between the two.

THIRTY-THREE

Spin Driftin' (B Side of Walls Come Tumbling Down, 1985)

Paul and The Jam

A guess this, but maybe this song was written as an answer to all those who came to Paul with earnest looks and tape recorders and opened up the interview with the question, 'So why did you break The Jam up?' That was the question Paul heard all the time, the one that masked his achievements since the band's break-up.

This song, with its rolling acoustic guitars and slightly rushed vocal line (so as to give the song urgency), is another underrated one. Paul talks a lot about himself here, how he knows he should be grateful, but that that in itself isn't enough, and sometimes the best get bored, as he did in The Jam. Later, he tells us he could have stayed for ever and a Sunday, just waiting, watching the world go by, all for the sake of being reasonable.

Many of his songs from this period talk about his wish to grow, to find himself, to live his life as he sees best. This is never easy, he tells us, but at least it is an honest kind of living. Paul has always been strong-headed, stubborn, purposeful. He has never needed much advice to direct him on life's path; he has his own sharp antennae for that purpose. Given his career longevity, they have served him awfully well, despite the wishes or complaints of others.

THIRTY-FOUR

Call Me (B Side of Come To Milton Keynes, 1985)

Paul and Family

On first hearing this song, I naturally assumed it was a lover's declaration, the message all lovers down the centuries have sworn to each other: I will always be there for you. Not so. Paul told me he wrote this as a parent speaking to a child – and this long before he had any children of his own. It is a good song, and one that explores the most important influence in his life.

John and Ann Weller gave Paul much; from Ann comes his drive, from his father his fighting spirit. Both lavished inordinate amounts of love on him, made him the very centre of their lives. Both made sacrifices, too, so that he would not go without. They have been hugely important role models, especially John, as he managed Paul from day one. It was a unique set-up, without parallel in British music. To give you an idea of the depth of their relationship, consider this quote from Paul: 'If my dad was to pack it up, I would seriously consider quitting myself.' That is not the Paul of today, of course. That is twenty-four-year-old Paul, his future still in front of him – just after The Jam had split up, in fact.

John Weller was born in Brighton on 28 November 1931. His family moved around a lot, eventually settled in Chichester, Sussex. At school, John took up boxing, excelled at the sport. He fought as a welterweight in the Southern Counties Championship and the ABA Championship, and also represented England. He was one tough fighter. Dean Powell, who works for the promoter Frank Warren, is also a huge Weller fan. He was chatting one day to Dave Stone, an old pro, and asked him who in his career had been his toughest ever opponent. 'That's easy,' replied Stone. 'This guy I fought years ago called John Weller. I hit him and I hit him and I hit him, but I could not put that man down.' (Dean recently engineered a reunion between the two men.)

John left school at fourteen and worked briefly for the *Chichester Observer* as a junior reporter (ironic, given his distaste for the current practitioners of the noble art), but the wages were low and he quit. In 1949, he was called up for National Service. He served three years in the army as a physical training instructor, won the services championship for boxing. When he was twenty-four his parents moved to Woking. John found work at a local factory, and he also found Ann.

They were married on 31 March 1957 at Woking Register Office. In 1958, their first son, John Paul Weller, was born. A daughter, Nicola, followed in 1963.

John and Ann doted on Paul. Neither had enjoyed close family relations when they were growing up, so it was natural they pour all their stored-up affection into their first-born. In doing so, they instilled in their son a huge sense of self. 'If a child only has to yell for someone to come running to minister to him,' Anthony Storr observes, 'it must be easy for him to maintain the illusion that he is at the centre of the universe.' Say hello to Paul. The self-belief that courses through his veins was put there by his parents. He later recognized the bad side of their mollycoddling of him, but as he always persuasively argued, 'How can you blame someone for loving you too much?'

John's main employment now was as a hod carrier on building sites, though he worked in various professions. There were many weeks when he was 'knocked' for his wages, meaning he wasn't paid. For the first eighteen years of Paul's life, lack of money was a big issue (an issue that did not unbalance Paul as it gave him a massive chip on both shoulders). The family was close-knit, defensive, insular. There weren't many other relations, so they closed ranks. An us-against-them mentality was created, one that would be highly influential when father and son entered the music business. I remember standing next to John and Paul in a bar the night before his famous Glastonbury show in 1994 and hearing them speak about the headliner Elvis

Costello as if they were ordering a hit on the man. Which, metaphorically speaking, I suppose they were.

In 1972, Paul and his close friend Steve Brookes played their first gig together at Sheerwater Secondary School. They then went about putting together a group that Nicky, Paul's sister, would name The Jam. John got heavily involved in the band from the outset. It was he who would hustle the band gigs, badger pub and club landlords. He landed the boys their first ever public gig at the Woking Social Club because that was where he and Ann went every Saturday night. It was John who hired vans to transport equipment, John who pulled strokes. In 1974, for example, he got a contract to build an extension at the local prison, HMP Coldingley. John gave the prison two quotes. The lower offer included a condition that they allow his band to play to the inmates and that they be allowed to invite the press along for the occasion. The prison granted them the request, and as a result The Jam got some of their first ever press.

'He was vital in terms of encouraging us to keep on doing it,' Paul recalls, 'and more importantly, he was vital in getting us gigs and motivating us to play live. There were loads of times when we could have split up, but he always pulled us back together again.' Steve Brookes said of John, 'John was two hundred per cent dedicated to getting the band off the ground and poured all his time and much of what little money he had into it . . . if the musicians in the band were the bricks, then John was definitely the mortar that held it all together. I doubt very much if the band would have gone so far as it did without his dogged perseverance.'

Yet it was John who showed real doubt when Polydor signed the band. To put it bluntly, he felt out of his depth. Booking pubs and clubs, a doddle. This was something else. He tendered his resignation to the band. They of course refused. John hooked up with Clintons, a firm of lawyers, and they guided him through the minefield of contracts and hidden clauses. He learned quickly, learned that the more you got up front, the more they had to work to get it back.

John's management style was to put everything into his son, to take note of no one else but Paul Weller. This stance threw up some funny stories. When Noel Gallagher offered his band as a surprise support slot at one of Paul's Manchester shows, Weller liked the idea and told Noel to get his agent to call his father, arrange the details. Oasis had just hit the big time. They were everywhere. Their debut album was number one, they were on TV and radio constantly, and on the cover of every magazine. You couldn't move without seeing a picture of or hearing about Oasis.

Noel's agent called John, told him Oasis would be up for supporting Paul.

'Oasis? Where they from then?' John asked.

'Manchester,' said the agent.

'Oh, local band,' John replied. 'Give them fifty quid then.'

John supported Paul in everything he did, even if he vehemently disagreed with it. He loved The Jam and spent time trying to persuade Paul not to break them up while, in 1988 he had no idea why his son had suddenly started writing classical overtures, and then disco music the following year. He dreamt of Paul headlining at Madison Square Garden, a venue to which as a boxer he was greatly attracted, and spoke about it often. Paul shrugged his shoulders. He was never that interested in breaking America. John saw the business as a money-making operation; Paul had another agenda he wanted to follow.

'I have never had to write for money,' Paul once told me, and that was his father's greatest achievement: collecting enough moolah for his son to indulge his every whim.

That conversation took place in the mid 1990s, in a hotel, on tour with Paul. Afterwards I went downstairs and found John in a reception room, staring gloomily into a fire.

'Hey, John,' I said, sitting down opposite him, 'you OK?'

He looked up at me, serious concern written across his red-cheeked face.

'Here,' he said, 'do you think I've been a good manager for Paul?'

The abruptness of the question caught me absolutely off guard.

'I mean, I've played it really straight with him. You know, album, tour, that kind of stuff. You don't think he would have been better off with a Malcolm McLaren type?'

I wasn't lying when I told John that he was easily the best manager for Paul Weller. Apart from the fact that a McLaren-type regime, full of scams and stunts, would never have suited Paul's nature in a million years, John's drive to earn money gave Paul what he needed most: total artistic freedom. The riches he piled up in banks for his son allowed Paul to follow his muse wherever it took him. In the latter half of the eighties particularly, Paul ended up in some fascinating places. The fact that he was so musically diverse is, I would say, John's greatest achievement as his manager.

Certainly without him Paul struggled. In 1995, days before the band were due to fly out and start a Japanese tour, John Weller fell gravely ill and was taken into hospital. He needed heart surgery. Paul was given the chance to cancel the tour but decided to go ahead, probably on the grounds that this is what his father would have wanted. (Some years later, in Liverpool, when Paul's drummer Steve White was called back to London following his brother's death, I asked Paul when the rearranged gig would be. 'Oh, we went ahead and played it,' he replied to my surprise. 'We did an acoustic set. The show always goes on.') His father's welfare was not the only upsetting element on that tour. One of the musicians Paul had picked to play in the band was clearly out of his depth, and it showed every night onstage, thus adding to the man's irritation. He couldn't even lose himself properly in his music.

One night, as he sat in my hotel room with me and the director Pedro Romhanyi, who was making a video of Paul, his frustration reached boiling point. He picked up a massive armchair and smashed it through the double-glazed window. All of us bolted. The next day the management took Kenny Wheeler, Paul's minder, to the room to show him the damage. Kenny tried to explain Paul's actions. He was simply picking up the chair, he said, and slipped. Unfortunately, as he did so he lost control of the chair, which fell through the window. An unfortunate accident, but these things happen. Really, said the manager. So how do you account for that? he asked, pointing at the marks on the room's ceiling which had obviously been made by chair legs being scraped across it. Ah, said Kenny, and reached for his chequebook. The room was on the fiftieth floor and a crane had to be brought in for repairs to take place. The cost probably swallowed up the tour's profits.

Funny now, but at the time Paul was badly shaken. The idea of working without his father had become a reality for the very first time. John recovered and spent many more years on the road, until he retired.

My favourite memory of John is this. We had booked into a hotel in Italy, and as it was such a nice afternoon, Paul, his father and I went out to get a coffee. We found a café in a park and sat down at a table. As the autumn sun began to dip, John gave us his thoughts on many subjects – his worldview, if you like. Paul and I just sat there and absorbed his words, his wise insights born of experience. It was the best half hour I ever spent with John Weller.

Ann, too, has a warm heart. When I interviewed her for my Jam book, she asked me questions about myself. When she heard that I'd lived in a children's home in Woking, she said, 'Oh, you should have said. You could have come and lived with us.' Although she had had a tough start in life, she was not the complaining type. She just got on with things. This is the way of the world, this is how it operates, no good moaning about, get on with it. Ann was a cleaner, and even when the money rained in she carried on with her part-time jobs. Still does today.

Ann is far more sociable and gregarious than John. She likes people, has a wide circle of friends and is compassionate to those less fortunate than her. Her principles have had a huge influence on Paul's development – it is why he works so hard. Between her spirit and John's determination lies a large part of Paul Weller.

THIRTY-FIVE

Have You Ever Had It Blue
(Single, 1985)

Paul and the Absolute Beginners Culture

When Paul lifted the Absolute Beginners title from the writer Colin MacInnes's book for The Jam's 1981 single, he had not read the book in question. When he finally did so, he was absolutely gripped. *Absolute Beginners* is Britain's first youth novel, a cool and hip journey through the life of a young nameless photographer who is into clothes, jazz, scooters and hip talk. Given those elements, you can see why Paul would have identified so strongly with this work. This was the Mod movement caught in its infancy.

Despite my suggestions, he never did buy the film rights. Instead, Palace Pictures, by then Britain's hippest film company, entrusted director Julien Temple with the job of bringing it to the screen. The idea made commercial sense. Jazz was a strong presence in

London's air at the time. Artists such as Working Week and Courtney Pine were attracting a lot of attention, and DJs such as Mark Murphy were creating a small but significant scene whose influence was being felt in the fields of music and fashion. Paul was never that knocked out by this scene – or indeed by contemporary American artists: I recall us in 1982 going to see Wynton Marsalis at Ronnie Scott's, and after three numbers Paul announcing, 'Well, this is a pile of shite,' and upping and leaving – but by donating a song to the film's soundtrack he got to work with the album's producer, Mr Gil Evans.

Evans is something of a legend, the man who worked with Charlie Parker, Gerry Mulligan and the great Miles Davis, with whom he made his name producing several landmark albums such as *Sketches Of Spain* and *Porgy And Bess*. Evans also created his own significant albums, such as *Out Of The Cool*.

Weller's song for the film was first premiered, according to Style Council archivist Iain Munn, on a 1984 tour. It was then put to one side until the recording of the album, *Our Favourite Shop*. Drummer Steve White had written an impassioned polemic against the Tory-inspired Youth Training Scheme which Weller placed the music from this song behind. He then resurrected the original for the 1986 film soundtrack of *Absolute Beginners*. Weller's lyrics homed in on one element of the character's story – his strong yearning for the love of his life, Crepe Suzette – and posed a series of ideas such as waking up to find the morning hasn't come, watching the day go by with your feet tied to the floor, and the girl you want ignoring the one love that really is worth fighting for.

The song was so much better than the film, which never lived up to its promise. I remember being at Solid Bond Studios when producer Steve Wooley turned up with a rough cut to show Paul. We watched it in a room at the back of the studio. Within ten minutes it was obvious that the work was a mess – badly acted, directed and scripted. We watched in shocked silence. The film finished, Wooley took his video out, looked at Paul for his response. Paul didn't say a word, just wished him goodbye. Wooley went home.

Paul turned to me and said, 'Oh well, at least I got to work with Gil Evans.'

THIRTY-SIX

A Stone's Throw Away
(*Our Favourite Shop*, 1985)

Paul and Politics (Part Two)

The album this song was written for, *Our Favourite Shop*, was a complete one-off. In the glossy musical climate of the 1980s, pop had lost its biting edge. Most bands avoided any sort of political statement. Either they had nothing to say or their many advisers counselled against making their positions known. The only causes bands were encouraged to take up were those that played on people's guilt, not convictions – hence Live Aid.

Paul, a product of the sixties and punk attitude, played the opposite card. No band was as anti-Thatcher as The Style Council, and it was this album that marked the height of their venom. The first six songs concern themselves with the effect on Britain of Thatcherism. Homebreakers looked at families torn apart as fathers sought work miles from home; All Gone Away detailed the closing down of towns and villages as a result of the economic slump; Come To Milton Keynes was a sarcastic jibe at that town's public image; Internationalists was agit-prop set to a funky wah wah guitar; and The Stand Up Comic's Instructions was a biting look at racism in humour.

But it was this song that topped them artistically. When Paul wrote 'political' songs, he utilized three lyrical styles. There was the call to arms – Walls Come Tumbling Down is a prime example. There was the biting sarcasm approach, exemplified by songs such as The Eton Rifles and Come To Milton Keynes. And then there was the more poetic approach, where Weller took a step backwards and was able to employ a more subtle, fruitful line. To accompany his meaningful sentences – how liberty must always come at a price and today's was the leather cosh breaking bones; that wherever honesty was to be found so too were scores of broken ribs – Weller used baleful classical-style strings and a strong vocal, to telling effect.

It was in 1985 that Paul got involved with the Red Wedge movement, which brought together musicians with the aim of encouraging audiences to vote, and vote Labour. The setting up of this alliance necessitated many meetings at Labour Party HQ in Walworth Road which Paul and I attended. It soon became clear that Paul was not cut out for such meetings. His was the direct way: do this and do that. These meetings got bogged down in tedious details. When the tour finally hit the road, Paul attended many press conferences where he found himself out of his depth as questions rained down on all sides, and he simultaneously began to develop a great suspicion about the motives of the politicians who aligned themselves to the cause, as well as some of the people instrumental in creating the movement.

Typically of the Left at that time, there were murmurs of discontent about Paul's stylish way of dressing. One day at a meeting Paul turned up and handed out leaflets he had drawn up the night before which depicted a well-dressed man with the slogan COME AND JOIN THE F.O.P.S. above his head. And typically of the Left at that time, although the 'S' certainly stood for 'socialists', no one got the joke.

Seeing the Labour Party up close – the in-fighting, its intransient nature, its inability to move fast, and above all its Machiavellian use of celebrities – put Paul off party politics for good. After Red Wedge, his only political statements were of a more general nature, such as speaking out against the invasion of Iraq or bemoaning the state of the NHS. Paul would always argue that in practical terms Red Wedge had done some good – opening up youth centres, for example. But perhaps the best thing to happen to Paul during this time was that he saw The Smiths play on one of the Red Wedge tours, and for the first time in ages reconnected to the kind of power great live music can convey. The last band he had seen do that was The Jam.

THIRTY-SEVEN

The Stand Up Comic's Instructions
(*Our Favourite Shop*, 1985)

Paul and Humour

Music was not the only art form to adopt a determined political stance in the 1980s. Through the arrival of a new generation of comics, comedy began the process of self examination and ridding itself of its bad habits. Lenny Henry was a major force in this movement, attempting to carve out a humour that didn't rely on sexist insults or racial epithets. By the time of this album, Henry had made a lot of headway in his quest, and he was the perfect choice for Paul to bring into the studio to recite this dialogue between a club owner and a young comic.

This is one of the very few dialogue-heavy songs that Paul committed to vinyl (he never liked records that featured talking, *à la* the soul singer Bobby Womack, who would often break off to have a little *tête à tête* with his listeners) and was done in the style of a comic talking to his audience and adopting different characters. The story is simple: the club owner tells the new kid what sells to the audience, the racist one about the Irishman, the Asian, etc., and the young comic recoils in disgust. The title itself feels like a John Osborne play.

Paul has never been publicly associated with humour, and that does the man a disservice. The image of Paul as a humourless being stems from his encounters with the press. So wary is he of what he says, of what will be reported, that he rarely relaxes, therefore his humour never shines through. Plus, he takes his work extremely seriously. Yet the fact remains that Paul can be very funny when the mood takes him.

Paul likes humour of almost every hue. He is a fan of Benny Hill, and of saucy comedies such as those British *Confession* films Robin Askwith made his name with. He likes Ealing comedies, too, but also contemporary humour: he is a fan (with reservations) of programmes such as *The Fast Show*. He can also be quite filthy. Once, in the Jam days, a bunch of them defecated into a newspaper and tied it under the chair of a prominent record company boss.

He likes humour that debunks people, earthy humour. He loved the story I told him of when Michael Jackson brought his pet chimpanzee on to the pitch at Fulham and the fans started singing 'I'm forever blowing bubbles . . .' He also enjoyed the story of the Millwall fans shouting 'Play Going

Underground!' to the Burnley player Paul Weller.

His tastes are wide, although the American smart-gag genre pioneered by shows such as *Frazier* and *Cheers* he never ran with. He prefers catchphrases, loves making puns on words. 'Modernists?' he said of a bunch of badly dressed boys we passed by on a coach one day. 'Sodomists more like.'

He is also quite cheeky. The Who biographer Chris Charlesworth once approached Paul to ask if he would be interested in writing sleeve notes for the CD release of The Who's first album. 'No, I wouldn't be,' came back the reply. 'But I'll re-do the vocals for them.' 'Are you still a spokesman for a generation?' *Melody Maker* asked him in 1984. 'Nah,' Paul coolly replied. 'Just part-time now, evenings and weekends only.'

Many view the public Paul as dour. That's because he is either making or promoting his music, the most serious job in the world. Outside that arena, Paul Weller can certainly have his moments.

THIRTY-EIGHT

A Man Of Great Promise
(*Our Favourite Shop*, 1985)

Paul and Dave Waller

If Steve Brookes was the closest to Paul's heart, their
friendship uncorrupted by fame and fortune, then Dave
Waller was closest to Paul's soul. It was Waller who
introduced Weller to art and poetry outside the mainstream. He gave Paul challenging literature written by
the Beat writers Jack Kerouac, Allen Ginsberg and Ken
Kesey (whom Paul liked best of all). Waller also introduced him to Bob Dylan, and directed him to that
man's magnificent lyrical power. 'At the time,' Weller
once told me, 'I was still writing June and moons, sub
Beatles rubbish, and Waller was writing about political
things or himself or about pain. He was much more
advanced than I was.'

Weller was always grateful to Waller for doing this.
It has already been noted that he published one of

Waller's poetry collections, *Notes From Hostile Street*, through his Riot Stories imprint; he also included a poem about him in The Jam's songbook, entitled Letter to Dave Waller. In it, Weller states that Waller's words gave him new hope for the future, that society should kneel down and pay homage to him, and that he remains a loyal and devoted friend, number one in the Dave Waller Fan Club.

I had just begun hanging out with Paul when Dave Waller died from a heroin overdose, and I was struck by Paul's seeming indifference to this terrible event. 'Do you remember that guy I used to hang out with, Dave Waller? Kicked it, didn't he,' Paul told me one day at the Townhouse Studios in West London, where he was recording the Jam album *Sound Affects*. And that was it. I knew they had been close, but Paul seemed simply to shove everything under the carpet.

Of course, he had been affected. I just didn't know at the time that he would find fuller expression for his grief in this great song. Paul's understanding of his friend is quite moving: he sees his death as tragic, a great promise of talent unfulfilled, but he is astute enough to know that maybe Dave Waller (like Liza Radley) would always have been a troubled soul, one that forever burned brightly but refused to settle, and that maybe he is happiest now, six feet under, with no one to bother him.

THIRTY-NINE

Waiting (*Cost Of Loving*, 1987)

Paul and the Road Less Travelled

In recent interviews, Paul has begun admitting to issuing 'dodgy records', but always with the caveat that at the time of their writing and recording 'I meant it'. And he did. I know from personal knowledge that whenever Paul embarks on a course of action, he does so with unwavering commitment. Time might prove the idea wrong, but never the force behind it.

If there is one period during which a surfeit of 'dodgy' songs appeared, it was 1986 to 1990. What caused this drop in standards? Many are the reasons.

Love was one. In 1984, Paul and Gill Price separated for good. The final parting happened on a tour of Japan, and so loud were the sighs of relief within the Weller camp, they could be heard from Tokyo. With that tempestuous relationship laid to rest, Paul moved to a flat near the Solid Bond Studios. Within the year, he and Dee C. Lee became serious lovers, eventually marrying in 1988. (They did so at a register office in Basingstoke. As the vows were being made, Dee began to cry tears of joy, and Paul responded by laughing. As his wife's tears increased, so did his laughter. It was a funny and touching sight.) The intensity generated by their love proved overpowering. Dee now replaced music as the main obsession in Paul's life. For the first time in some years, he lost interest in his band, in work, in writing. All he wanted was to be with her, and all she wanted was him.

In hindsight, the obvious move would have been for Paul to have a lengthy period away to develop this all-important relationship, then to return fresh and ready. After all, he had kept up an amazing pace in The Style Council, writing or co-writing nearly fifty songs in just over two years, many of which resonate today. But there were factors working against such a move.

The main problem was a financial one. To keep the studio they had bought back in 1984 open, Paul had to make an album a year. The idea to attract other bands to work there when Paul wasn't recording, and pay the rent, was always ridiculous. Very few bands liked Paul and his high opinion of himself, and no doubt Paul had publicly castigated them somewhere down the line. The only musicians who recorded at Solid Bond – The Blow Monkeys, Young Disciples, Ocean Colour Scene – were either friends or huge admirers of Paul. The rest of the musical world spent their recording budgets elsewhere. To cover the bills, a record advance from Polydor – said at the time to be worth a million an album – was crucial.

At the same time, Paul had become fascinated with contemporary American soul music. He now decided to emulate it by making an r'n'b album. Not a commercial one that harked back to the sixties and the raw sound of Motown and Stax and Atlantic, but one that carried a modern-day sound, full of drum machines and synthesizers. Dee C. Lee, who had spent much of her youth in soul clubs, was an obvious influence here, as was Paul's liking of singers such as Anita Baker (whom he offered his song Walking the Night and was very disappointed when she turned it down), and records by Alexander O'Neal and the Valentine Brothers (the latter appear on the album).

Rock music held no interest for him at this stage. 'I think a lot of it is attitude,' he told *Smash Hits*, 'but I don't like the sound anyway, the big thrashing guitars and that macho, "we're all boys together" thing. I find this attitude clichéd and very boring and negative.' Of the leading acts of the day, the U2s and the Echo and The Bunnymens, he said, 'They are embarrassing, so dated. I find them cynical and think they are really smug groups.' Paul now stopped playing guitar on stage and instead danced his way through live sets.

But his true way of expressing himself is through song-writing, and the word 'love' now started turning up frequently in his songs and song titles. Sweet Loving Ways, The Cost Of Loving, All Year Round, and this song, Waiting, released as the second single from this album and the first ever not to make the charts. The song is listless, it glides along aimlessly, though Paul has a lot of time for it. 'I think this is a really underrated song,' he once told me. 'I think it's a really beautiful song. The chords are fantastic. For me, it's Stevie Wonder influenced. It was also the first tune where we knew we were on the slide because I thought this was a top tune and it didn't do anything.'

Paul had come a long way, from angry young man to crooner, and the lukewarm reaction from his audience to such material was the first sign of a restlessness that would increase over the next few years. Not that Weller seemed to mind. His stubbornness, essential to all artists, drove him on. 'The more they found it difficult, the more I played on it,' he later admitted to *Mojo* magazine. 'I make moves because they interest me at the time.'

FORTY

How She Threw It All Away
(*Confessions Of A Pop Group*, 1988)

Paul and The Beatles

I always took this song to be about Gill Price, how if she had played her cards right she would still be by Paul's side. However, in an interview with *Mojo* magazine, Paul said of this song:

Can't say where it came from or what it was influenced by. It's me with my professional head on, writing a tune. There's that element when you have to finish a record and although there might be half a dozen songs which come from the heart you have to write another six or so and where are they going to come from? You can't wait around forever, which is good I think because although sometimes they might end up workmanlike other times you can come up with great songs and I think this is an example. I think it's a really good pop record but totally out of sync with what was going on at the time.

It's notable too for its use of the Beatles song title Can't Buy Me Love, although Paul inserts an 'I' into the line so as to make it sit properly. That move always bugged his designer and friend Simon Halfon. He, like Paul, was Beatles obsessed. Together, he and Paul would chase down any bootlegs, books, memorabilia – anything to do with the band in fact. This also extended to mimicking the band's distinct Liverpudlian accents. Paul once told me, 'You remember those solo albums The Beatles put out after they had finished? That no one bought? Well, that was me buying them, even Ringo's.'

This dedication to The Beatles has been a constant in Paul's life. 'In the art rooms at school,' classmate Steve Baker recalls, 'there were pictures of The Beatles everywhere with slogans such as WE LOVE THE BEATLES underneath them. Everyone knew who stuck them up.'

For Paul, there were definite mystical energies around The Beatles. Not only were they incredibly talented, but their look had been crafted from above. 'Look at the way they have perfect symmetry in all their onstage pictures,' he used to say to me. 'Because Macca is left-handed, both guitars point outwards.' (He thought the same of The Small Faces, their short heights creating a unique look.)

Paul, Simon and DJ Gary Crowley were the only ones I knew in the 1980s to carry a torch for the band. No one else I knew talked about them, raved about them, with such intensity. I too love the band, but I'm not so reverential. I once dared to go on Radio London and argue that the *Sergeant Pepper* album was not the band's greatest hour, and in fact should be pulled up for starting the decline of the single. On my return home I was basically drummed out of the regiment for my insubordination. I am still reminded of this piece of rank treachery. 'Leave *Pepper* alone,' Paul once said to me as if discussing one of the seven wonders of the world.

In the 1990s, The Beatles became hip, a turn of events which of course triggered Paul's cynicism, especially the vast coverage given to the band by the monthly adult music magazines. 'There's nothing more to fucking write about them,' he would fume, 'yet they've done another piece on them.' Then I would notice a copy of the magazine tucked away somewhere.

'Paul?' I'd say, holding it up.

'Well, what can I do?' he'd reply resignedly. 'I'm a fan.'

FORTY-ONE

It's A Very Deep Sea (*Confessions Of A Pop Group*, 1988)

Paul and Self-examination

If the sun was a symbol of positive force in Paul's work, then water was a dark, mystical force. Three years earlier he had likened his inner confusion to drowning in the River Seine in the Style Council song Down In The Seine. Now, in order to view the mistakes of his past he was diving into oceans to find himself. Paul was aiming to dive so much that eventually the sea itself would drown, and dry land (peace) would be found. Regret is a theme that runs through much of Paul's writing; as Anthony Storr tells us, the creative person is far happier dealing with people and problems through art than he is in real life (see Porcelain Gods). And water fascinated Paul. I recall being on holiday and him staring wistfully out at the Mediterranean, expressing his wish to write a piece that would capture its soul.

This was in the late eighties, by which time Paul's listening tastes had turned towards the classical world. He liked a lot of Debussy's music, also the French composer Erik Satie, whose introduction into classical music of a minimalist sensibility Paul found absolutely compelling. Jazz-wise it was the Modern Jazz Quartet (see The Peacock Suit), whose vibraphone-led music tended to be as clear and as cool as water in a stream. All this put Weller as far away from rock music as possible, and if his journeys into hitherto uncharted musical waters blew him off course at times, it also elicited from him some of his greatest songs, such as this piano-led ballad about self contemplation.

Paul writes well on piano. His melodies are rich and lush, and highly resonant. (In fact, an album of his piano songs would be a great way to expose this side of his songwriting and challenge people's image of him.) This is a song that rises above musical genres. It has lightness in its touch and beauty in its soul.

Yet despite this beauty I have to ask, was Paul at this point hell bent on making Polydor Records' life as hellish as possible? And if so, why? Look at the situation from their point of view. They were allegedly paying him a million pounds an album, and what does he give them? An r'n'b album inspired by obscure American indie soul music, *The Cost of Loving*, followed by a classically led album, *Confessions Of A Pop Group*, and, in 1989, *A Decade Of Modernism*, an Acid House album. Meanwhile, for the first album he insists on an orange cover (inspired by The Beatles'

White Album) and on the second he fights tooth and nail to have his picture on the cover removed – a battle he loses.

In the first years of The Style Council, Paul strode out with his tongue in his cheek and a pocket full of songs, shouting the odds for all the world to hear. Many people thought him mad, and he delighted in their confusion. Interviews were full of spark and humour, videos that mixed the pretentious with the colourful were encouraged, adverts full of wind-ups to both press and audience appeared, and life was an unfolding adventure. Early Style Council music reflected that fresh and invigorating approach. Five years down the line, boredom set in, gripping the whole operation with an inertia mirrored by the slow pace of many of Weller's songs at this point. A dismissive contempt for Polydor, a growing insularity within the Weller camp and Paul's belief in following his musical heart put paid to the bright sparks of the loafer-heeled boys.

As we know, his 1986 single Waiting was the first of his never to chart. Paul just shrugged his shoulders. What the fuck. In 1989 came *A Decade Of Modernism*, his take on Acid House music, which still hadn't reached the mainstream. Polydor refused to release it. Their argument was that they were haemorrhaging money on the band and wanted music they could sell. Arguments erupted. 'I'm not used to being talked to like that,' Weller later said of these arguments. The writing was clear for all to see. Fuck you, Polydor said, and ripped up his contract.

The man who had been gainfully employed as a musician for twelve years, who had become a national figure and a hero to thousands, was now out of work. He went home, confused, angry, defiant. He looked after his son, and faced the nightmare of all creative people – writer's block. It would take him two years to get out of it.

There is a counter argument to all this which simply asks, shouldn't Polydor have realized that a man capable of writing a song as great as It's A Very Deep Sea is a man worth persevering with? That in the long run it would be highly beneficial to allow him the leeway to explore his musical obsessions because one day he would find himself and reward them handsomely?

Paul did just that for the record companies he later signed with.

FORTY-TWO

Into Tomorrow (Single, 1991)

Paul, Success and Spirituality

His first solo release and important single, this. Weller had been out of the loop for two years, and despite his previous success he now found himself at the bottom of the pile, which confirmed his lifelong cynicism about the music business. They love you at the top, but at the bottom? They don't hate you, it's worse: they ignore you.

His first solo tours played universities, small clubs. The line-up he chose reflected his uncertainty: sometimes he took to the road with backing singers and brass, other times not. This really was a bad time for Paul. As a man who had spent all his life knowing exactly where he wanted to go and what he wanted to be, to be gripped by confusion and uncertainty about his future was highly unnerving for him. Weller's reluctance to open up and share his worries created the illusion that he thought as I did: that given the longevity and depth of his work, it would only be a matter of time before the creative juices sparked up again. But I was wrong. Paul was going through a real crisis at this juncture.

I realized this on one of his first solo tours, when one afternoon in my hotel room Paul sat on my bed and suddenly blurted out, 'I don't think I am an artist. I don't think I am a songwriter.'

I looked at his face, saw the very real worry shooting through his eyes, and I was stunned. If there was anyone I knew who *was* an artist, it was this man. If there was anyone who *could* write songs, it was this man. He had been doing it for thirteen years now, sometimes tumbling, sometimes ascending, but always with his eye on the prize. Now, so fragile was his mindset that not even the quality of his back catalogue could convince him of his worth.

'Paul, don't be so silly,' I said. 'How can you not be an artist? Look at the musical journey you have made. Look at the songs you have written, how much you have changed. You've gone from In The City to It's A Very Deep Sea. You don't do that if you are not an artist.'

'I know, I know,' he said, but I could see he wasn't convinced. My words of encouragement could not assuage the desperate feelings gripping him inside. That kind of worry can only be killed by the worrier.

At the time of these very real doubts, the musical

world was spinning on its head (see Walls Come Tumbling Down). The Ecstasy revolution of the late eighties had ushered in a new sense of musical freedom. Rock and soul, always so far apart, began to draw closer. So did other musical genres.

There was something in the air, and around Paul's Holland Park house that something was marijuana smoke. He had reacquainted himself with an old teenage habit. Paul took to it enthusiastically. A friend of mine heard him being interviewed on the radio about three years ago. When asked what he liked doing to relax, Weller apparently replied, 'Listen to music and smoke a spliff.'

'And thank you very much, Paul Weller. Of course, younger listeners are advised . . .'

It was strange to see Paul imbibing the pipe. Up till then drugs had been kept at arm's length. Dope was smoked by hippies; cocaine was taken by decadent, irrelevant rock stars. As Paul hated both camps, these habits were deemed highly unworthy. What I didn't realize was that Paul worried about drugs, in the sense that he might become obsessed with them.

'I want to steer clear of chemicals', he told me. 'I think I have probably got an addictive personality.'

Certainly marijuana had an effect on Paul's writing around this time, as did age and fatherhood. These elements helped to shape a new philosophical Weller, one ready to look at every aspect of his personality. In the course of this journey into self-examination Weller visited a therapist, although he was never going to stick that particular course. 'I had a couple of sessions with a psychotherapist,' he told *Uncut* in 2006, 'I think I went home and thought, fuck it.' I wasn't surprised. Paul Weller is a man who finds it hard to open up to himself, let alone anyone else. Still, a process of self examination was seriously under way, and this search for a new direction was mirrored in Paul's lyrics.

In this song, the words show us where Paul has been as they speak about the joy and pain in learning, the tears and the searching, about the mists of time and space, while at the same time cleverly name-checking two major sixties soul clubs, The Mojo in Sheffield and The Twisted Wheel in Manchester. Musically, his breakthrough had occurred when he came up with this song's memorable riff, which he then set to a danceable beat, led by a booming bass and drum rhythm. (Increasingly in the first half of his solo career, many of his songs were given club mixes by his long-time producer Brendan Lynch.)

It was a fine comeback song. Noel Gallagher talks about seeing Paul at Brixton Academy at this time and how this tune stood head and shoulders above the rest of the set, convincing him that Weller was still a force to be reckoned with.

And he was right.

FORTY-THREE

Above The Clouds (*Paul Weller*, 1992)

Paul and Anger

The subject matter of this song is highly typical of the material Paul was writing at the time, endlessly questioning himself and the world around him, constantly seeking answers, solutions. In the past, life was so much easier. The world was black and white. This was right, that was wrong. You knew your way. Easy. Now the world is colour; now differing points of view can no longer be ignored.

A minor example of this was the change in Paul's listening habits. By his own admission, Paul never listened to any band or artist who had long hair or a beard. Which meant no Neil Young, no Traffic, no Nick Drake. As the English philosopher Herbert Spencer once remarked, 'There is a principle which is a bar against all information ... which cannot fail to keep a man in everlasting ignorance – that principle is contempt prior to investigation.'

Ironically, the lyric which is of most interest here (and I am not talking about the one inspired by Sam Cooke's A Change Is Gonna Come – compare Weller's 'when you're scared of living but afraid to die' to Cooke's 'it's been too hard living but I'm afraid to die') is located in the song's middle eight, where Paul makes mention of his anger.

To put it kindly, Weller has a short fuse, a fearsome temper – again, another characteristic that puts an immediate distance between Weller and those close to him. In fact, such is his volcanic nature, one of our nicknames for him was The Modfurious. Another was Hurricane Weller. His anger could flare up at any time, turn in an instant. There was not one person close to him, apart maybe from his father, he hadn't threatened or been verbally violent towards. At any point in his life, there is always someone for whom he harbours anger.

His anger was frightening, but it could also be unintentionally funny. Once, at a gig, a fan shouted something to him about the lackadaisical nature of the show.

'It's not my fault,' he snapped back, 'I've been on the piss for two days.'

Driving brought out the worst in him. Countless times I have been in his car conducting a pleasant conversation when all of a sudden Paul starts screaming 'What the fuck are you doing?' at someone, usually followed by the normal quota of effing and See You N T words. Then he would turn to me and say, 'Sorry, what was that you were just saying?'

Paul spat fire at everyone, sometimes for the flimsiest of reasons. He had a go at me once for being on TV too much. He nearly fell out with another close friend because of his liking of a certain band (see Walls Come Tumbling Down). In public, the most famous example of his anger was when he exchanged words with the Sex Pistols bass player Sid Vicious, and cracked a glass over his head. The reason for the argument has never been disclosed, although the fact that the Pistols' single at the time, Holidays In The Sun, carried a similar riff to The Jam's debut single has caused many to suspect this to be the crux of the dispute.

Anger infused much of his music, even his 'ballads', where he often inserted a section to quicken the pace, or fired in some angry chords from nowhere. Paul hates it when things are getting too cosy. Music was, in fact, a good way for him to channel his anger. Punk, for example, provided him with a great opportunity to let off steam on his guitar, as does much of the music of his solo career.

Where did this anger come from? Some would point to Paul's upbringing and money almost constantly being in short supply. I don't buy that. Others have been through far worse than he could ever imagine and emerged *sans* fury. No, I think it was passed on from his father, the boxer, this need to obliterate the opposition or be obliterated. It is an attitude Paul took into the music business. Take, for example, his recent spitting on a picture of Sting at the Royal Albert Hall. He did so because Sting's music had 'no edge, no attitude'. Yet Paul wouldn't spit on a pic of Pavarotti or Tony Bennett, and their music has no 'edge' or 'attitude'. So could it be that Sting's huge success is the real cause of Weller's anger – when the world listens to Sting, the real problem is that they are not listening to Paul Weller? What really riles Paul is that Sting does not obey the standards he has laid down. Paul believes music should be created and performed in a certain way, and his is the right way. No other argument can exist.

The Sting spitting incident is indicative of something else: Paul's mission at the age of forty-nine to show that he is still an angry young man, that he hasn't lost it, gone soft, that he is still fulfilling one of his favourite lines of poetry, Dylan Thomas's advice to 'rage, rage against the dying of the light'. (Whether the poet had gobbing on pics of rivals on his mind at the time I'm not so sure. You will have to go above the clouds to ask him as he passed away on 9 November 1953.) Paul hates the process of ageing, and it is helplessness in the face of it that often provokes the fury.

He recently slagged The Clash off to a friend of mine, which means Paul Weller must be the only man fighting a war that finished well over thirty years ago.

FORTY-FOUR

Everything Has A Price To Pay
(B Side of Above The Clouds, 1992)

Paul and the Art of Songwriting

As the process of self-searching continued, it was not long before Paul began to examine that which was of most importance to him – songwriting. One of Paul's greatest impulses is always to demystify, to hold things up to the light and rip away all pretence. Songwriting is no different. Although many place songwriters in a romantic tradition, see them as damaged souls waiting for the muse to visit them, Paul strongly disagrees. For him, songwriting is a job. It is his work.

'I've got a family, I work for a living,' he barked at *Mojo*.

OK, he will tell you, some songs come to him as if from above, but this is the exception, not the rule. The majority come through hard graft, and he wants that to be made clear. Most people think he conjures up songs from nowhere, but this is wrong, he states, far off the mark. Songwriting is hard, difficult, requiring hours and hours of effort and worry. With each new composition you shoot into the dark, nervously wondering if people will like it, if the talent to dazzle is still there, or if your time is nearly up.

Paul likes to write at night, in his kitchen. He loves the idea that as the world is sleeping he is beavering away, creating magic ('At midnight's hour when the world is sleeping' he sang on Out Of Sinking, making a reference to this penchant of his).

How do songs come to him? Various ways and means. Sometimes a riff, a lyric, a piece of music will come to him from nowhere; other times he plays guitar relentlessly until something happens. My theory, based on what Steve Brookes tells us about their early days with The Beatles songbook, is that one way Paul writes is to play other people's songs on his guitar until they mutate into his own compositions. Sometimes he thinks of ideas he can work on, such as Wings Of Speed, where he hit upon the notion of marrying the style of an English hymn with an American gospel feel. It was then that he began work on the song. Of this act of creation, composer Aaron Copland noted, 'it must either be entirely spontaneous, or if not spontaneous, then cajoled, induced, gradually perceived, so that each day's work may spell failure or triumph. No wonder many creative artists have been reputed to have had unstable characters.'

Our very warm and intelligent friend Anthony Storr

249

places creative people in several different categories. Paul, what a shocker, has elements pertaining to many of these types. First, there is the creative person as schizoid (let us not forget Paul's quote in the introduction about his girlfriend calling him psychotic). This is someone who is preoccupied with the inner self. 'An individual with this chemical structure,' Storr says, 'gives an impression of coldness combined with an apparent air of superiority which is not endearing.' This is Paul on playing a festival where the group REM were also appearing: 'I'd never watch a band like that. No, I didn't talk to them. They talked to me.' You may recall how John Entwistle bored him, 'so I gave him my autograph and went home'. The advantage for this songwriter or artist, Storr continues, is that they get to choose what they reveal. 'He cannot be betrayed into confidences which he might later regret. He can choose (or so he often believes) how much of himself to reveal and how much to keep secret. Above all, he runs little risk of putting himself in the power of another person.'

The second type Storr recognizes is the creative person as an obsessional character. Money, for example. Why are most successful artists so tight with their money? Because, as we know, 'free spending is a form of letting go'. Obsessionals have a compulsive need to control 'both the self and the environment', and Paul certainly controlled others, while resisting every attempt to control him. (These musings on his character will absolutely enrage him, as will every attempt to pin him down. 'I don't recognize myself in any of the interviews I do,' he once said, which I think tells us more about him than inaccurate journalism.) Paul feared change, too, not particularly in himself or his music, but in those around him. He confessed this fear to me on a couple of occasions. His major worry was that people would change so much they would become different characters who would then walk away from him, hence his insistence on loyalty to the cause. You are either with or against Paul Weller. No middle ground exists in this battlefield.

Obsessionals also 'look ahead in order that they may not suffer the anxiety of the unexpected' – another aspect of Paul's character we have already had cause to touch on. Paul was forever thinking of the future, pencilling in provisional tour and recording dates, making endless plans. He doesn't like surprises. The world is too un-stable for his taste and planning ahead is one way of imposing some kind of order on it.

His passion for all things Mod ties in with these characteristics (see The Peacock Suit), as does his neat-ness. In every house of his that I visited, I never once saw a room of his majorly cluttered or untidy. There were always neat rows of records, clothes, books or any other items to be seen. Storr mentions the observations made of the desks the composers Stravinsky and Rossini worked at. 'It is probable that the extreme orderliness of the desks and the tools of the trade,' he writes, 'is an outward and visible sign of the order which these composers wish to produce in their com-positions.' And indeed the world: a dislike of dirt is another symptom of this type. 'Dirt is commonly regarded as disorder,' Storr explains, 'as something alien which has intruded itself into a system . . .'

Storr then moves on to the creative ego, observing that independence is of paramount importance to the artist. 'This shows itself particularly in the fact that they [the artists] are much more influenced by their own inner standards than those of the society or the profession to which they belong.' The expectations Paul had of himself were always huge. He rarely satisfied himself, and when he did, the feeling was fleeting. Every song had to be better than the last, every song had to mean something, every song had to say something memorable. This takes a heavy toll, he tells us in this key song. Paul shot for his moon so that he could reach the stars. That journey is not for free, he reminds us. There is a price to pay, and I pay it.

Maybe, one finally wonders, that price is happiness. 'Writing is not a profession, but a vocation of unhappiness,' the French author Georges Simenon once said, before adding, 'I don't think an artist can ever be happy.'

FORTY-FIVE

Remember How We Started
(*Paul Weller*, 1992)

Paul, Dee and Happiness

Paul's relationship with Dee was the first to expose him to true love, deep love, and it elicited many songs from him. Some were wonderful, such as Changing Of The Guard (a classic), some were deceptively intense and catchy (Sweet Loving Ways), some were mournful (Walking The Night). In many of them, Paul stated and made crystal clear his greatest wish, which was to return to the halcyon days of their early relationship, when they lived in a bubble and were absolutely consumed by their love for each other.

In the documentary *Into Tomorrow*, Dee makes the most interesting observations about Paul. The first is her revelation that Paul was obsessed with happiness. 'He kept on saying, "Is this real? Are we allowed to be this happy?" '

Why would Paul fear happiness? I think for two reasons. Paul's emotional scale, as with every true song-writer, is wide. Not every human has this quality. Some are dominated by an emotion which takes precedence over others – sadness or anger, for example.

Paul doesn't have this problem. He experiences and understands many emotions, knows how to tap into them through his music. In his work, anger, fear, insecurity, joy, outrage, contentment and, yes, happiness all jostle together. To allow one emotion to supersede all others would therefore be to tamper with the DNA of his make-up, and seriously interfere with that which is most precious to him, the writing of songs. If he was happy all the time, how would that affect his craft? It was a dangerous question, one Paul did not want answered. Better to let all emotions exist at the same level and keep safe the mystery of the song-writer's ability.

Secondly, I think a fear of total and lasting happiness, a condition that surely all humans aspire to, could stem from his class's culture – the idea that you should never get above your station, be that financial or emotional. This was a common notion among the British working class of the 1960s and 1970s. 'What are you looking so fucking happy about?' is a phrase common to a million council estates. As with the alcoholic who must be surrounded by drinkers so as not to have his behaviour challenged, so the miserable and the unhappy drag you down to their level, make sure you do not get above your emotional station.

Lyrically, this song carries some of Paul's trademark telling details – the moonlight shining through Dee's flowered curtains, the way she turns his head so that they can melt into their first kiss – while musically, the song's guitar pattern echoes his Style Council song *Waiting*. As we have seen with the similar chord progressions of *When You're Young* and *That's Entertainment*, much of Paul's music is a work in progress, a constant search for true expression. It is also a reflection of his listening habits at the time, Paul judiciously mixing disparate elements, a haunting refrain taken over by a Donald Byrd-like workout.

For quite a few people, the *Paul Weller* album remains their favourite of his solo work, probably because the musical influences are unique and allow Weller the chance to expand musically without finding himself on such dreaded terrain as prog rock, or worse.

FORTY-SIX

Amongst Butterflies (*Paul Weller*, 1992)

Paul, Nature and God

Tony Blackburn once asked why Paul couldn't write about the nice things in life – the birds, the bees, the fields. Fourteen years later, Paul took his advice.

Whenever an artist heads out in a new direction, he worries hard about his audience accepting it. Yet it was vital for Paul that he stay true to his instincts, that he strike out for pastures new. In this case, it was nature he now began to examine with poetic vigour, and this Sly Stone-influenced song was one of his first stabs at it.

Following in the tradition of Tales from the Riverbank, this is another homage to the countryside Paul played in as a child. In this case he is thinking of the woods near his old home in Stanley Road, where a statue had been erected to honour the contribution of

Indian soldiers in the Second World War. (It got into such a state of disrepair that Paul privately offered twenty grand to have it restored. Overjoyed, the owners made public Paul's offer and in a fit of temper he withdrew his proposal.)

In such childhood-tinged songs, Paul always sought to replicate the magic he felt as a young innocent. He wanted to touch upon the magnificence that had touched him. But now he also wanted to know deeper things, such as where had this magnificence come from?

When Paul spoke of God in his songs, which was a rare occurrence, it was usually to link the Church to the hypocrisy engendered by its link with the Establishment: vicars waving boys off to war, churches groaning with gold while the poor go begging, that kind of thing. Weller instinctively shunned organized religion, its churches and its rituals. He thought it all hypocritical. Yet he did believe in a God, had done so for a long time. This is him talking to *Melody Maker* in 1982: 'It's very difficult when you start talking about religion because everybody thinks you have gone a bit nutty. I don't belong to any particular religion, but I do believe in God, as such.'

Paul's belief in a higher force was probably ignited by his love for and awe of nature, and strengthened during the course of writing songs such as Wild Wood, which seemed to flow through him. This intense feeling, that a power is conducting itself through a human vessel, is nothing new to musicians. American jazz drummer Art Blakey has spoken of it, so has Keith Richards, and many others. It was a feeling strong enough to convince Weller that God's wish for him, his purpose on this earth, was to provide music.

God now became much more of a presence in Paul's songs (see All Good Books). He is manifest here in the lovely image of a whisper upon the breeze. This sensitivity towards nature was always in Paul, but dope smoking had probably helped bring it to the fore. As for his audience, they too were having similar experiences and feelings as they aged: the birth of children, which in turn triggered a spiritual questioning, followed by a growing need to explain the world and their place in it before time called time. No wonder those young bucks at the music press thought up the term 'Dad Rock' to pillory Weller with. He didn't care, nor did his loyal audience.

FORTY-SEVEN

Sunflower (*Wild Wood*, 1993)

Paul and Extra Duties

I first heard this one Friday night in 1993 at the Manor Studios in Oxford. Paul loved this studio. Set deep in the Oxfordshire countryside, the Manor was the perfect place for Paul to work and to play. One could blitz one's head here on booze and chemicals, or one could soothe one's soul by the deep lake or in the dramatic countryside. One could work like a demon or party like a madman. Of course, Paul did all this and much more.

The night I heard Sunflower I commented on the song's blistering opening guitar riff. Paul told me how he got the intro. 'I was practising this guitar scale,' he explained, 'and then for some reason I reversed it, and that's the riff.'

What a clever boy, I thought.

Years later, I heard a song by a sixties band called Les

Fleur De Lys entitled – and I kid you not – Gong With The Luminous Nose. I realized that the guitarist in the band had hit upon exactly the same idea as Paul thirty years earlier. Amazing. What a coincidence.

On one of his tours of Japan, Paul had found himself in the whirlpool of a mad relationship. The heat between these two was the same as when you meet your lifetime partner. Yes, it was that intense. In normal circumstances they would probably have stayed together for years, but Paul was a touring musician. That's why they have 'no future', they have 'no past'; they only have now and their intense feelings. This record captures that intensity and is important in that it set a musical attitude and template for much of Paul's forthcoming music. This is the record where it sounds as if he is finally letting go of all inhibitions, launching himself towards destination unknown. Where before he had been badly under-produced, now his sound was as big as the feelings he was trying to capture. It was a major breakthrough.

FORTY-EIGHT

Wild Wood (*Wild Wood*, 1993)

Paul and the Orphans

In 1994, after purchasing Black Barn Studio in Ripley, Surrey, Paul spent a lot of his time commuting from London in his car, a beautiful blue Mercedes SL Pagoda Roof his father had purchased for him for his thirtieth birthday. As you travel up the A3 towards London, if you glance to the right you will see a drive leading up to a house. Clearly visible from the road stands the name of that house: Wild Wood. Paul noted that phrase on a regular basis until inevitably its suggestive imagery triggered his creativity.

The song was written in the kitchen of Paul's house in Holland Park, late one night. It is one of his finest compositions, a song that seems to have flowed through him. There is not a note out of place, nor one false move. This is as close as you will get to some kind of perfection within the man's body of work. That's because Wild Wood has a simplicity about it that is compelling, hewn from a plaintive guitar riff, a hushed foxtrot rhythm and a beautifully poised vocal.

When it came to recording the song at the Manor Studios in Oxfordshire, Marco Nelson was present. He had recently read that the musician Tom Waits had recorded one of his songs in the open air. He told Paul this and it was decided to try Wild Wood in this fashion. Equipment was set up outside the studio on the lawn and the band ran through the song a few times. The recording was not to Paul's liking, however. He felt it was too dry sounding, so the band (Steve White on drums, Nelson on bass, producer Brendan Lynch on mellotron, Paul on vocals and acoustic guitar) headed back inside where the song was recorded in the conventional way.

The day I first heard this song was memorable. It was during the filming of the documentary I was working on about Paul, *Highlights and Hangups*. Paul had just written it, and when Paul has a new song, especially one as strong as Wild Wood, he always wants to play it and get a reaction. He approached director Pedro Romhanyi and offered to play the song on electric guitar for the cameras. It was the song's first ever public airing. He settled on a stool with just an electric guitar and began the song. About halfway through the performance I felt a tear come to my eye, the very first time one of Paul's songs had affected me in this way. At the song's conclusion, I had to look away. Why was this?

Because, as Paul later explained, he had written the lyrics partly with me and his then wife, Dee C. Lee, in mind, both of us having been dealt terrible hands at the start of our lives.

Interesting to note how three people who had been through varying degrees of trauma as children – me, Dee and Steve Brookes – figured strongly at points in Paul's life. 'I'm so lucky,' he told Q magazine in 1993, 'to have had such a loving family. Most of my friends have had nightmares growing up.'

I first told Paul about my upbringing over coffee in Hyde Park in the summer of 1983. By his own admission, Paul didn't know how to react to my story of parental abandonment and children's homes, two issues that are obviously (and thankfully) outside most people's comprehension. In his thirties, however, as Paul started to delve inside himself, he came to see how his own loving and secure childhood had given him many positive qualities which had been crucial to his happiness and success. Foremost among them was an unshakeable confidence in himself and his talent. The song Wild Wood was a product of this confidence and talent, but also of his compassion for those for whom life draws a bad hand. It was Paul reaching out to us all.

Wild Wood acknowledges the pain, the confusion, the darkness, but it does something else: it makes a beautiful promise of redemption, tells of a golden rain that will come one day bringing all the riches that are so deserved. (The traffic image at the song's opening, incidentally, was inspired by the cars Paul saw every morning clogging up Holland Park Avenue – 'high tide, mid afternoon, people fly by in the traffic's boom'.) As always with Weller, there is advice, too: 'don't let them get you down, making you feel guilty'. And then, salvation: 'You are going to find your way out of the wild wild wood.' They are striking lyrics.

Fittingly, the album this song came from was Weller's biggest hit in years; Wild Wood itself hit thirteen in the UK single charts. Paul recalled how proud he was driving down Wardour Street one afternoon and hearing this song fly out from another car's radio – a moment of high self-satisfaction for the man. The song's classic nature broadened his audience and brought critical acclaim. But more than that it bolstered Paul's musical confidence. He had written a classic song, one that transcended his influences.

I can pay no higher compliment to this song than this. In 1996, I spent a year writing and researching my first Oasis book. I lived, listened, drank and ate nothing but Oasis. And then the work was finished, and I could emerge from my self-imposed cocoon and play whatever I liked. I looked at my large record collection, and I reached for this song.

FORTY-NINE

All The Pictures On The Wall
(*Wild Wood*, 1993)

Paul and the Hindsight of Lovers

Weller's debut solo album, *Paul Weller*, did not sell in vast numbers. At the time of its release – it went in at eight in the charts – I was visiting newly discovered family in Sorrento. Paul and John arrived for a few days' break. This entailed sunbathing during the day and drinking heavily at night (see There Is No Drinking). On about the third day there, Paul and I were walking through the hotel courtyard when John opened the window of his bedroom, called down to Paul. He had been speaking to the record company and had news of the album's chart position.

'Oi, mush, album went down to twenty.'

I turned just in time to see the disappointment flicker across Paul's face.

'What about next week?' he asked.

'They [the record company] are going to try and hold it, but you know how these things are,' John said, shrugging his shoulders in resignation. 'Anyway, thought you should know. What you guys up to?'

Two weeks later Paul was at his studio in Ripley furiously demoing new songs he had written. This was one of them, a minor classic, and proof that Paul is never more inspired than when he has his back against the wall.

The song was born in a pub, during a conversation with the landlady about the portraits of her ex-husband on the wall. This was something that fascinated Paul: how things change, how something that was once so passionate could be left hanging in ice-cold hangars of emotions. What happens to that love? Where does it go? Is its departure inevitable? If so, is that the fate that awaited him and Dee?

These are the kinds of questions hinted at in this compelling song, a mature look at life's often capricious ways set to an insistent running acoustic riff that mirrors the pace of love in its first flushes and a tempo which then reveals and remarks on its slowing down.

FIFTY

Foot Of The Mountain
(*Wild Wood*, 1993)

Paul and Music

Much to his frustration, Paul could never take full control of Dee C. Lee. Every time he thought he had her pinned down, she slipped out of his grasp – like a dream on the ocean, he wrote of her, always moving away. It was this quality of Dee's – her unpredictability – that kept Paul chasing, kept Paul fascinated. She was the one he could never quite capture, and that frustration drove this song into being.

Musically, it adopted the style of Neil Young, evoking one of that man's most famous songs, Heart Of Gold, with its chopping chords. Paul became infuriated with this comparison, even though he had clearly written *in the style of* Neil Young. And that was never made clearer than when he played this song live, turning it into a guitar epic which tested the patience of even his most ardent fans. He also began indulging himself with the song Shadow Of The Sun. His musical journey had allowed him to make this transition from the short sharp shocks of The Jam to guitar workouts such as these. Paul's playing was never that showy off, though; rather, he sought atmospherics and expression in his playing. In fact, such was his passion for this style, the length of both these songs in live performances became talking points for the fans. After every show they would post on the web how long both songs had lasted, comparing the time to previous shows.

This emphasis on technique and playing has become something of a recurring shout of Weller's. When I expressed my surprise, for example, at him choosing Toploader to support him, he retorted sharply, 'Well at least they can play their instruments.' This stress on musicianship is a fallback used by many musicians. It covers up their insecurities and doubts about their own work. It also gave the anti-Weller press ammunition, as his stress on craft and discipline ran counter to their notions of music as a spontaneous expression.

Complex guitar workouts such as these are in many ways the culmination of a musical journey that began on Stanley Road, Woking. As a kid, Paul was mainly into pop; as a teenager, mainly soul and reggae. In The Jam, it was a few contemporary records (Pistols, Clash) mixed in with sixties beat bands such as The Kinks, The Small Faces, The Action. (When Edsel released a best of The Action LP in the early 1980s, Paul's sleeve notes and public support had much to do with the compilation's success.)

In the eighties, his tastes dramatically expanded. He became a big jazz fan, mainly the Blue Note variety. Blue Note music was perfect for Paul, not too abstract, not too mad. Many songs began with a striking riff which the musicians then developed over the course of the song. I remember Paul being a huge fan of a percussionist called Sabu, and his album *Palo Congo*. Later on, Paul got into some of the heavier stuff, people such as Pharaoh Sanders, John Coltrane and Charlie Mingus. The latter had a big effect on Paul. He bought me three Mingus albums for my birthday once, and in the card he wrote, 'This is a disciple giving you an old master.'

At this time, Paul also began to incorporate a Latin influence into his work. The songs of Everything But The Girl heavily inspired him. 'Paul, obviously, to be generous, listened hard to us,' Ben Watt of that band generously noted. Songs such as The Whole Point Of No Return, Come To Milton Keynes and All Gone Away testify to this influence.

Modern soul tunes became an obsession, too. Booker Newberry's Love Town was a big tune for Paul, as was Glen Jones's I Am Somebody, and Osiris's War On The Bullshit. Then there was the Invictus label, set up by the Motown songwriters Holland, Dozier and Holland in 1967, their genius in creating a bridge between soul and pop unabated. The work of The Chairmen of the Board in particular was highly attractive to Paul. Theirs was soul with edge and meaning, but sweetened by great songs and melodies – perfect for his outlook. (Paul would remix Lover Boy, a General Johnson track, in the late eighties, but he didn't do a great job.) David Sea's Night After Night exerted a massive influence on the third Style Council album, *The Cost Of Loving*.

Naturally, the established artists were also investigated: Stevie Wonder (Paul was big on his *Where I Am Coming From* album), Marvin Gaye, James Brown, The Isley Brothers, Sly Stone, George Clinton.

Paul liked hip hop, but only if it carried a positive message – the work of Tribe Called Quest, for example. He especially liked Gangstarr. The radical black politics of, say, Public Enemy he found a barrier, as he did their theatrical live shows ('What's all that about, then?'). He hated the braggadocio of much hip hop.

Acid House he grew to love after first dissing it. 'I much prefer Council House music,' he said in *The Face* in 1988, when asked about it. It was a flip comment, and not a smart move. The scene comprised working-class kids who had grown up on Weller, adored him. His dismissive quip upset a lot of them, and I should know because they would come up to me in clubs and continually ask about it. I made Paul a tape of some of the tunes, and then it clicked into place for him. Unsurprisingly, it was the songs that carried meaning that he homed in on – Someday by Cee Cee Rodgers, for example, with its great vocal and upbeat message. He loved Blaze. We went to Wembley Arena once to see them, though both of us decided it had been a waste of time to hear house music in that cavernous location.

House music was crucial to Paul at this stage in his career. After the bad reaction to the *Loving* album he needed to find a musical trampoline that would allow him to play on his strengths, and house music gave him that opportunity. He could be modern, relevant and not have to resort to angry guitars. He would, of course, go on to make a whole album's worth of Acid House – the one Polydor famously turned down.

The first rock record, if we can call it that, that caught Paul's ear in the late eighties was There She Goes by The La's. Even though the pair of us were at this point listening exclusively to black music, Paul got that record straight away. 'It's got something very special, that song,' I recall him telling me, 'something really good.' In the 1990s, Paul invited The La's to support him at one of his Shepherd's Bush gigs. They arrived with little or no equipment, went onstage at 7.30 and despite frantic calls from the management refused to leave it until they had played out an instrumental as long as a motorway.

In fact, the late 1980s and early 1990s saw the strict lines that had separated black music from white begin to blur. Maybe it was the result of the Ecstasy boom, which saw personal and social barriers crumble to the ground. The playlist now became a mix of soul and rock. Esther Phillips's Home Is Where The Hurt Is was a big tune, as was God Made Me Funky by The Headhunters; The Young Disciples' debut album *Road To Freedom*; the work of Alice Coltrane, especially her song Journey in Satchidananda, which Paul unwittingly put on three different tapes he made me, so enthused was he by it; Bobby Hutcherson's Ummh; and The Cool Out by Leroy Hutson. Mixed into this bed of black music was the work of songwriters such as Tim Hardin (especially the song It Will Never Happen Again), Nick Drake (The Riverman), Gram Parson (Paul loved his song White Lines), Van Morrison and, in particular, Neil Young and Traffic. Just listen again to the live version of this song, Foot Of The Mountain, or Clues from his first solo LP, to see the effect of these artists. ('Great,' quipped a rival manager. 'It's taken him ten years to get from 1966 to 1969!')

The wave of British bands that defined the late 1980s, the Stone Roses and Happy Mondays, never touched Paul in the way it touched the younger musicians he came into contact with, such as guitarist Steve Cradock. He also had reservations about a lot of the Britpop bands, homing in instead on specific songs, such as Don't Look Back In Anger or Shakermaker by Oasis, and Blur's To The End. He was also flattered by the homage these bands paid him.

There was of course a huge amount of music Paul dismissed out of hand, which always left one suspicious because the person or band in question was the competition, the enemy. Certainly there were a couple of occasions when I was amazed at his dismissive attitude, especially towards class acts such as the Liverpool band Shack – the work of songwriter James Roberts. Often I felt his dislike was not on musical grounds but for personal ambitions. He once remarked that when he rented a flat in Holland Park owned by U2's bass player Adam Clayton, he should have got it 'for free as U2 nicked all the Jam fans' – which explains a lot about his perspective on some bands.

Of late, Paul's enthusiasm seems to be for new bands. In a recent *Daily Telegraph* feature he chose a top ten of records he was currently grooving to: The Arctic Monkeys, Dirty Pretty Things, The Kooks, Graham Coxon, Yeah Yeah Yeahs, Dr Dog, Declan O'Rourke, Guillemots, and Tunng, a folk ambient electronica act. He also revealed his great admiration for the Libertines song What A Waster. And why? 'Because I've been trying for years to fit "two bob cunt" into a lyric and actually make it scan right,' he revealed, with customary panache.

As in everything, Paul is a perfectionist. Every element of a record has to work for him – the words, the melody, the playing. One detail out of place and Weller turns off. He was Stalinist in his approach to music. In the mid eighties I began to write a lot about hip hop. I loved the funky nature of many of these tunes, the playful and often poetic wordplay. For Commissar Weller, however, even if the music was amazing, if the lyrics weren't saying anything of value, he simply wasn't interested. I can recall him being scathing about so much music, like the Oasis single Do You Know What I Mean?, simply because of a verse that quoted Bob Dylan and The Beatles. That was it. That one verse made the whole song redundant. I loved

Dexys Midnight Runners beyond sense; Paul couldn't abide them. Paul loved Syd Barrett; I never understood him. I was for Springsteen, Paul firmly against. He was against much landmark American music – Arthur Lee's Love, for example, or The Velvet Underground. (Many of his most virulent critics – Steve Sutherland, Allan Jones – were huge fans of the music Paul disliked.)

Paul and I agreed on a lot of subjects, but yes, we had our musical differences. I was never as hateful about bad music, though. Paul's animosity could be venomous. On a couple of occasions he actually came close to falling out with people over musical prefer-ences. In the late 1990s, Paul began to refer to music as 'his religion'. It was music and its surrounding culture that he worshipped. To him, music was a sacred, spiritual force that should not be cheapened by com-mercial considerations (such as television adverts).

But just as he hated, so he loved. In the end, as I often told him, music is an ocean. Just when you think you have heard it all, something rolls up to amaze and surprise you. Paul Weller will sail that ocean for the rest of his days.

FIFTY-ONE

Moon On Your Pyjamas
(*Wild Wood*, 1993)

Paul and his Children

This is Paul's first song for one of his children, in this case his first-born, Nathaniel. It is a composition whose subject matter was probably inspired by the John Lennon song Beautiful Boy, which had become a favourite over the years. Weller's song is not in that league, though, for it borrows too heavily from the Rod Stewart song Tonight's The Night. The song's main image was inspired by a mobile that hung above Nat's bed and cast moonlike shapes on him as he slept.

Lyrically, Paul, always on the alert for cliché, tries to avoid sentimentality by widening the song's scope: it is rare, he confesses, that he makes wishes, but he so hopes the world heals itself so that his son can grow to see its beauty. He hopes love and laughter will follow him everywhere, for his presence has made his father see life with new eyes. Pretty sentimental stuff, right?

Adults tend to repeat their childhood experiences. Paul, as his parents did with him, dotes on his five children. He is a hands-on father, highly protective (such was his desire to procreate, I used to call him the Fela Kuti of London). Children are special to Paul. Their existence alone is proof of higher forces, forces beyond our comprehension. 'Whenever I look at my children,' he once said, 'I see the face of God . . . If there is anything good and worthwhile and positive in the world, you see it in a child's face.'

Nat was born on 10 May 1988. The night before his birth, I stayed at Paul's house. In the morning, he entered my room. 'Come on,' he said, 'We're going to the hospital.' Next thing I knew we were in a waiting room. Several people came and went during the day. Nat finally came to earth in the early hours of the next morning. Paul came into the room and said, 'It's a boy.' As he embraced his father and me he was visibly moved.

In his teens, Nat adopted a goth style – a fashion a million miles away from Paul's very personal Mod style. Although Paul branded the music 'appalling', he was obviously pleased that his son was into music and had made encouraging noises about forming a band. It was a striking sight to see them out and about in London, as if Steve Marriott had just bumped into Marilyn Manson.

Leah came next, and for her Paul wrote the song Sweet Pea, placed on his *Heliocentric* album. An affair with a make-up artist named Lucy produced another girl, Dylan, born on his birthday, 25 May. I was with Paul when the news of her birth came through, at the old CBS studios in Whitfield Street. The first thing Paul did was to walk from the control room and into the studio where he sat playing the piano for a good twenty minutes.

While recording at Manor Studios in Oxford, Paul met his current partner, Sammi. With her he has had two children: Jessie, the subject of You Who Brings Joy, placed on the *Illumination* album, and his best 'child' song by a mile; and Mac, his fifth child and second son. No doubt he will draw out a song from his father at some point.

Paul is in constant communication with his offspring, spends as much time with them as possible. He is completely in tune with the Brian Wilson song Child Is Father To The Man. He loves it when one of his children chides him, tells him to stop being so miserable. And he often finds himself siding with them even if it is wrong to do so. I recall him telling me once how Nat had told him how much he hated school and never wanted to go back. 'I was exactly the same at his age,' he said, 'but I can't tell him, "You're right, son, school is crap and a waste of time." Never did me any harm never going in, but I can't say that, can I?' But you could see how pleased he was with his son's independent stance.

FIFTY-TWO

Country (*Wild Wood*, 1993)

Paul and his Secret Location

This is one of my favourite Weller ballads, a song that
continues the romantic theme of The Jam's The Place I
Love, Paul guiding his lover towards a secret place, a
destination only he knows about, where life's sweet
perfume hangs in the air. What's impressive about the
lyrics is their maturity. Weller anticipates a time of great
happiness to come for him and his lover, but only if
they are somehow able to lose their discontent: 'and
further on we'll find a time and lose the discontent we
feel'. It was a feeling he would have noted but probably
not spoken about with his wife. After all, his
relationship with Dee was, unbeknown to both of
them, entering its final phase, so the lyrics take on a
deeper meaning. Unusually for one of his 'slowies',
Weller allows the song to flow at its stately pace

without inserting too many dramatic flourishes. Hidden away on *Wild Wood*, this precedes the album's other great song about his first wife, Foot Of The Mountain.

FIFTY-THREE

The Changing Man
(*Stanley Road*, 1995)

Paul and Contradictions

Bit of a kerfuffle about the origins of the title. An acquaintance of Paul's, Terry Rawlings, told Paul he was now managing a band called The Changing Man. He claims this is where Weller got the title. Paul firmly disagrees. The title had come from his daughter Leah, three years old at the time. 'Leah had this funny little doll she used to carry around with her,' Paul explained. 'I said to her, "What's that you got there?" And she said, "It's the changing man." I thought, "That sounds great, I'll put that in storage." ' This explanation is very similar to how John Lennon got the title for Lucy In The Sky With Diamonds.

In the opening line of this song, 'Is happiness real or am I so jaded', Weller is once again questioning the assumption that success leads directly to personal fulfilment. Everywhere he went at this time, people seemed to be telling him the same thing: 'You must be really happy now.' The *Wild Wood* album had taken off. In a week it had sold more than the collected sales of his previous album, *Paul Weller*. The quality of its songs, plus his upping of the ante at live performances, had got him back in the charts, back on TV and radio, back on the covers of music papers and magazines. From playing tiny clubs and student halls at the start of this phase of his career, he was now booking the Royal Albert Hall for three- and four-night stands. It was impressive stuff.

Yet Paul was far from happy. Why? Because his personal life was a mess.

One of the more interesting things to come out of the *Into Tomorrow* documentary was Dee C. Lee's observations on the change in Paul around this time. She pointed out how the Weller of the 1970s and 1980s – the man from The Jam and The Style Council, the man she had married – kept adulation at a distance. Nice to receive, but never to believe. Now he seemed to be taking these compliments on board, acting more and more like a rock star, forever taking things to excess. In truth, Weller had decided to let loose and enjoy himself as much as possible. The years of denial and guilt were to be put to the sword. He was now going to take all on offer and sod the consequences. Time was starting to make him feel his own mortality and Paul wanted everything he had previously refused. The things he had once despised, he now loved. 'I used to feel terribly guilty about everything,' he said in 1992. 'The money, the lifestyle, the hotels and stuff. Now I think that I worked hard for it all, so why shouldn't I enjoy it?'

This is an important quote for understanding Paul's psyche. It's an attitude backed up by a line from Shadow Of The Sun, from *Wild Wood*, in which he states his intention to have it all while he is still young. Paul was gradually shedding his guilt, refusing to feel bad, starting to display a bullish mood that would grow in strength over the years. His enjoyment now came in many forms. The use of drugs was one (see Porcelain Gods), as was his alcohol intake (see There Is No Drinking). The massaging of his ego was another.

A new generation of bands had now come through – Oasis, Blur, Stone Roses – who openly acknowledged the debt they felt towards Paul, not only in terms of his music but in the way he had conducted himself over the years. Suddenly, Paul was getting kudos not only for his past work but his current material as well. He began hanging out with some of these musicians. Noel Gallagher is the obvious example, but he cultivated links with many others, such as The Charlatans, Stone Roses and Primal Scream. Paul had never hung out with so many musicians. In fact, he had never hung out with musicians before. He had always avoided that scene. He found it cliquey, obnoxious. Plus he had nothing in common with any of his contemporaries. In the 1990s, that changed. When asked about this in 1995, Paul defensively responded, 'I don't feel part of some big music club – just because we play guitars, we're supposed to get on. It doesn't work that way . . . obviously.'

The process hasn't stopped yet. He is still doing it now, appearing on stage with the likes of Carl Barat from Dirty Pretty Things, offering his support to the likes of Hard-Fi, The Dogs and The Rifles, conducting duets with Amy Winehouse. This was such a different Paul from the one who entered the 1990s. His circle of friends widened considerably. He was more gregarious, more sociable, more out to enjoy himself while he still could.

The other major change in Paul's life at this time took place at home. The turning point was his appearance at the Glastonbury Festival in 1994. The following week, Dee C. Lee and he separated. She had discovered her husband had been unfaithful.

She had suspected this for a while, though. The night before the Glastonbury show I went to a Mexican restaurant in Notting Hill with Paul and Dee. I sat opposite her, and throughout the meal she repeatedly kept telling me, right in front of Paul, that if she ever found out that he had strayed she would not be responsible for her actions. On and on and on she went. Paul kept his head down, and I was screaming inside, 'Well turn to your left and tell him, not me!' But of course that was exactly what she was doing, telling him that the game was coming to an end, prepare yourself.

Anthony Storr neglects to make any link between success and sexuality in *The Dynamics of Creation*, but from my observations of such people, a high sex drive seems to be common to those who rise to the top, in whatever profession. The fact that he has fathered five children tells us much. To walk down Oxford Street with him was to watch a head in constant motion, left to right, back and forth, checking out mostly anyone female. In fact, I often used to kid him: 'Paul, Paul! Look, look! Check out the . . . ankle on her.'

In his 'I want it all and I want it now' mood, Paul had opened himself up to temptation. Women throw themselves at pop stars – fact of life. I have seen the most incredible-looking women alongside the most incredibly ugly men because they have a name in the public domain and a guitar round their neck. Paul took what was offered and he paid the price (see I Should Have Been There To Inspire You). He hadn't really done so before, so no wonder he sang about his changing character with such passion.

What is amusing about this song is that its opening riff was soon being compared to the main riff on Electric Light Orchestra's 10538 Overture. For Paul, this would have been as embarrassing as being caught stealing underwear in an old people's home. If you are going to steal and be caught, let it be from someone with credibility, not a bunch of old rockers from the seventies. 'I think the riff was Brendan's idea,' he told me in an interview a couple of years ago, swiftly passing the ball to his long-time producer Brendan Lynch, 'because he was using lots of samples and did a montage thing and out of that came the tune. It was his backing track. I had the melody and some lyrics already written and we put the two together.'

Weller's lyric writing style at this time veered towards a stream-of-consciousness method: he would write down anything that came to mind and then return to it later for any nuggets. He used this approach for the majority of *Stanley Road*'s compositions. 'I like that style because when I come back to it there is always something I can use,' he confirmed. 'It might be two lines, a phrase, a whole verse, and I'll write a whole song around that. Whatever is there, it forms a core, and I would say that applies to eighty per cent of the songs on this album. I like those sort of songs because it leaves a lot up to the imagination of the listener. The song isn't necessarily about one thing, so people can put what they like into the lyrics.'

FIFTY-FOUR

Porcelain Gods (*Stanley Road*, 1995)

Paul and the Dark Side of the Road

With its spiky recurring riff and confessional-style lyrics, Paul loved to refer to this song as a 'modern day blues'. It picks up from the Style Council song It Just Came To Pieces In My Hand, Paul again trying to shatter the illusion of invincibility that attaches itself to the famous. The chorus says it all, Weller presenting himself as a porcelain god, forever shattering.

The opening lines – more advice to fill up your head – seem designed as a dig at the culture of instruction that has grown up since the mid 1990s – experts telling you what to do, how to live, what not to do, what to wear, where to go, what to eat, how to act, how not to live, and on and on. For a blunt working-class boy like Weller, this was all too much, and certainly he was cutting loose.

Separated from his wife, Paul was now living in a mews flat (owned, much to his chagrin, by U2's bass player Adam Clayton, to whom he had to pay rent) near to his family home in Holland Park. It was the beginning of a period in his life characterized by a regular ingestion of chemicals. Until now he had steered clear of them. He had tried Ecstasy once – took a quarter of a pill on New Year's Eve 1990 at the Fez Club in Paddington, and nibbled on my ear for five minutes – but it was only in the mid nineties, when, as the musician Damon Albarn so succinctly put it, 'a blizzard of cocaine descended on London', that Paul really turned his attention to chemicals. Cocaine was his thing, as it was for many others.

In fact, the wired nature of so much of *Stanley Road* directly relates to its usage. This song, for example, is partly about paranoia, partly about cocaine, partly about fame – three very strong elements in Paul's life at the time. He later told me, 'If you take this song apart, every two lines mean something else or have a strong image to them. I like the opening lines – "Beware false prophets, take a stand / My fortune cookie cracked up in my hand" – those images are really nice. Then there is a bit about fame which could also apply to drugs: too much will kill you, too little ain't enough – both of which were going on at this time.' The part that drugs play in this album can not only be felt in the edginess of the music, but in his lyrics too. The lines in Porcelain Gods about 'playing games till dawn', for example, reflect that experience of seeing the night out on a sea of alcohol and chemicals, still talking as the morning breaks. He used to refer to the experience as being on the dawn patrol.

It is striking to reflect on the difference between the Paul of the Jam days and the Paul of the mid 1990s. 'What do you think of festivals?' he was asked by *Jamming* fanzine in 1978. 'I don't mind them so long as they are not drug festivals,' he sourly answered. In 1994, George Clinton, the leader of Parliament and Funkadelic and a seasoned campaigner on the chemical warfare front, walked on to Paul's bus at T in the Park, peered through the clouds of marijuana smoke, saw all the powders and pills, and exclaimed, 'Shit, I've been on the wrong bus all day.'

Paul eventually knocked cocaine on the head. He might have a little dabble now and then, but he has passed it up in favour of alcohol and marijuana. For Paul, the man always searching for meaning, cocaine was a porcelain drug, one that carried no substance. He would regularly complain to me about the bullshit words the drug made people speak.

Paul certainly needed his bullshit detector on him at this time. Most nights he went to sleep with his ears burning from people's praise. 'It was so full on, that period,' he recalls, 'because I was coming out from that period of time when I couldn't get arrested and now suddenly it was everyone going, "You're great, I've always loved your stuff!" Some of it was sincere but a lot of it wasn't, and I could spot the difference as well.' Thus his line in this song about people shouting out his name, and Weller calling their bluff. As one obsessed with the self, Paul knows only too well the flaws in his character. The later line about hating what others hated in him is spot on. Paul recognizes his failings, feels them all too keenly. He can be so selfish, so sharp-tongued, so moody, so hurtful and mean to those he loves; yet he is loath to change his ways because he does not want to tamper with that which made him, his talent for song-writing. He has always said to the world, this is how I am, take me or leave me, for I cannot force change upon myself. It has to come from within.

The paranoia inherent in the song's music is expressed in the final verse, in the statement that people are vultures; they will try to take everything away from you, and then watch you crawl. London was full of these types, and Paul had bumped into many of them. Even without them, Paul was paranoid about so many things, including his friends. I recall being absolutely devastated when in the mid 1990s, as we sat together in a bar in the Piazza Tasso in Sorrento (Paul loved the place, until he discovered southern Spain), he unequivocally stated, 'I don't trust anybody.' This after fifteen years of close friendship. But after a while, the hurt changed to sorrow – sorrow for a man who has to think in such a way. Wouldn't want to wish that on anyone, let alone another porcelain god.

FIFTY-FIVE

Time Passes (*Stanley Road*, 1995)

Paul and the Passing of the Years

Paul grew to be fascinated by the nature of time. It amazes him how quickly it seems to flow as the years pass, how it brings changes so subtle that one day you wake up and everything is suddenly different. 'Ever since my thirties,' he told me once in an interview about this song, 'the passing of time has fascinated me. I'm obsessed with it. My little girl Jessie is going to be five years old soon. Where's that gone? Those are the things which amaze me. It doesn't sadden me, it's just, where's it gone? It's disappeared into the ether. So it is a bit of a preoccupation and it crops up a lot in my songs. But this song is also about a personal relationship, splitting up with someone and then seeing them in the street years later, and how you still feel about that person.'

Time infuriates Paul, the way in which it affects the

body, robs you of youth and strength. We are helpless against its onslaught, which makes time a power we can never match. Paul doesn't like that, doesn't like it at all, but it is, of course, forcing him to look to his future, to wonder how long he has left both as songwriter and as man. 'Whether we like it or not,' he said in 2006, 'we are all getting older. You get a beer belly and you go grey and you get lines on your boat race [face]. Gravity will have its way, the way of all flesh.'

Time Passes is an elegiac ballad, piano-led but drenched in haunting guitar shapes which resound throughout, echoing the sentiments of the song, the sense of wonder and loss. Fittingly, it is a song of such high quality that it will withstand the test of time.

FIFTY-SIX

Wings Of Speed (*Stanley Road*, 1995)

Paul and Art

One of Paul's favourite pastimes – and one that over the years assumed a growing importance to his songwriting – is visiting art galleries. We went to many exhibitions together, including Peter Blake's Commercial Art Show (a real fave that one), a show of American landscape painters at the Tate, and any Pop Art show that came to town. Paul responded to art as he did to nature. It was a force of inspiration, a mystical power that acted as a catalyst for his own creations. In London, he especially liked the Tate Britain. ('Look at that floor,' he cheekily told Lesley White of *The Face* in 1984, in his clubbing days, 'great for dancing on.')

In 1994, on a visit to the Tate, Paul came across *The Lady of Shalott*, a painting by John Williams Waterhouse. He was transfixed by it. He still is. The painting was inspired by Tennyson's poem of the same name. In the story, a beautiful woman, the Lady of Shalott, lives alone in a tower. She is held in her room by a curse that does not permit her to go out or even look out of the window. Instead she can only see the world through a mirror. She spends her time weaving tapestries. When the handsome knight Sir Lancelot passes by her window, she is overwhelmed by him and, forgetting the curse, looks out of the window to see him. When she does, the mirror and the threads of her tapestry break.

She goes down to the riverside and finds a boat, and as she floats towards Camelot, she sings a song. As the curse works its evil magic, her blood freezes and she dies a cold death. The boat lands on the shore of Camelot and the people come out to see what has happened. They see that she has written her name on the front of the boat. One of the men in the crowd is Sir Lancelot, unaware of what has happened.

It is no surprise that Paul should be so heavily affected by this work. The painting brings together several art forms he is highly attracted to. There is the story itself, in which the character's romantic actions create ripples that in turn create more ripples. The fact that Sir Lancelot has no idea about his part in the Lady's death is a twist Paul would appreciate. Then there is the painting itself, a glorious example of the Pre-Raphaelite style, which Paul adored. Pre-Raphaelite art tends to be emotional and evocative, based in realism but imbued with an overt romanticism, an otherworldly spirit that elevates and enlightens the picture's essential Englishness. Paul has often adopted such an approach in his songs, taking the mundane and matter-of-fact and elevating it through poetry (see Town Called Malice).

The painting also represents a synthesis of art forms, which Paul always liked, probably because it was so redolent of the sixties. In that period, artists from all walks of life mixed, attracted by their keenness to experiment and their overt desire to break with the past. Example: Joe Orton writing for The Beatles, and Peter Blake designing their most famous album cover, *Sergeant Pepper*.

Throughout his career, Paul has made many attempts to marry his music to other art forms, such as cinema or TV. In 1984, he wanted to make a film to accompany The Style Council's second album, *Our Favourite Shop*. His idea was based around a quintessential Englishman, a sharp individual who runs a shop that contains only his favourite things, thus taking a stand against giant corporations. Nothing came of the project. Later there was an attempt at a musical, for which Paul imagined Jesus returning unrecognized to earth and no one taking a blind bit of notice. I started on a script for this project; Paul's job was to supply the music. He wrote one song which he played to me on the piano once at his Solid Bond Studios in Marble Arch. It was heavily reminiscent of another song whose name I couldn't recall. In truth, though, I was out of my depth, and I wasn't too surprised when the half-finished script was turned down by one of the Fox brothers.

In Wings Of Speed, Paul attempted to fuse two

musical genres. He wanted to imbue an English-style hymn with an American gospel feel. Paul often wrote songs this way, thinking of a musical idea first and then seeing if it would fly. In this case, he was on the button. He opens with a piano sound and style that carries distinct echoes of a morning assembly at a typical English school. Then his voice enters, cracked but also notably restrained, thus giving the song real emotional power as his words introduce the idea of the Lady of Shalott sailing towards him as he reflects on his personal limitations, restrictions only she can lift. 'I'll never be free / From the darkness I see / As I wait for your smile . . .'

To emphasize the song's spirituality, celestial backing vocals now enter, courtesy of Joy Hawley and Paul's long-time friend Carleen Anderson. Carleen spent three days preparing to sing her part. When she finally delivered, she said the sound came from her temples. That was how high she was reaching. At first the sound is unexpected, slightly jarring; but as the song flows you are moved by this mix of the human with the other-worldly – an (unconscious) fulfilling, then, of Pre-Raphaelite artistic ideals.

The result is one of his greatest and most moving songs, and I don't think Paul would disagree with that assessment. As far as I know he has never performed this song live, save for Jools Holland's show on BBC2. I asked him once why he had neglected it in the live arena.

'I think I would break down on stage and cry if I sang it,' he replied.

FIFTY-SEVEN

The Peacock Suit (*Heavy Soul*, 1997)

Paul and Clothes

Paul loves this record, with its tough musical explosivity, its defiant stance, its lyrics about Narcissus, the god of self, in a muddle, and the god Nemesis in a puddle.

Talking about music one night at Paul's house, I put forward a complaint that there weren't enough records about clothes.

'There's Peacock Suit,' Paul pointed out.

Music is Paul Weller's first and most glorious obsession. Clothes are his second. 'If you are from the working class,' Paul told *Mojo* magazine, 'then you know how important clothes are to our culture.' It has always been thus. 'He was the only trendy bloke in our class,' fellow Sheerwater pupil Steve Baker recalls. 'When you are eleven or twelve you are nothing, but he was trendy. When we were about thirteen, he was the fashion leader. We used to have a pair of loafers, and if you were lucky, a pair of Doctor Marten shoes. He used to have Doctor Marten shoes, loafers, brogues, Sta-prest trousers, Ben Sherman shirts, Brutus shirts, a Crombie coat, a parka, the lot.'

Paul has always been a dresser of distinction, his style drawn exclusively from the Mod tradition. He has never looked elsewhere for full expression. That is because Mod fits so neatly into the part of his psyche that demands control and order, cleanliness and exclusivity – and invites obsessive behaviour. As Storr noted, dirt is a no-no, and 'clothes must be neat and free from stain'. (A saying Paul often used? 'Cleanliness is next to Modliness.')

Traditionally, youth has expressed its teenage discontent through its appearance – think of the outlandish styles of teddy boys, hippies, punks, goths, etc. Mods go the other way. They dress to fit in. They don't want the attention, they don't want anyone to know what they are up to. This is why that great Mod Pete Meaden likened Mods to a guerrilla army. Mod has strict rules and regulations, prides itself on viewing the world in a completely different way to others. Little details, for example, are of paramount importance. Anyone can get the big things right; it's in the tiny flickers where the true test lies. Mod appealed to Paul's selfish and competitive nature. Many dislike Mod for its stress on one-upmanship; Paul loves it for precisely those reasons. From day one he has been gleefully trumping people with clothes.

Again, there is the contradiction to consider. In every account of his early days, Paul's character is gripped with shyness, almost to the point of inarticulacy. And yet, according to his classmate Baker, this retiring boy marches into school and draws attention to himself through his use of street fashion. Only one conclusion: clothes, like music, were for Paul a vital means of self-expression. What he can't say in words, he expresses through his wardrobe.

For some this proves shallowness within the character. Clothes are clothes, they are not of importance; there are other, higher things to consider. It is an erroneous assumption to make. Bob Dylan, one of the greatest artists of the last century, was recently photographed in Amsterdam. 'Make sure you get my shoes in the picture, that's all I care about,' he told the photographer. And so he should. The shoes were magnificent. Paul loves shoes as well. He is one of the best examples of that strict dictum which states that good dressing begins with the shoes and works its way up.

Paul's love of clothes created distance and confusion between him and the press. Their misunderstanding of his wardrobe drew them to the conclusion, much to his huge annoyance, that he was consistently changing image *à la* David Bowie. Not so, he shouted back. He was simply acquiring and trying out the wide remit allowed by the Modernist style.

Paul was a leader in the fashion stakes, both within his band of friends and in the world at large. I brought only two things to the table: the bowling shoes (I used to buy them from Melandi's when I worked on Carnaby Street, and Paul saw me wearing them one night) and the slicked-back hair look he used around the time of his single Money Go Round (I'm a big De Niro, Pacino, Soprano, Supino, anything ending in 'o' kind of man, so using grease in my hair was never the big no-no it is for others). That was it. Paul made all the other moves, I think.

In the early 1980s, immersed in cappuccino culture, we often met at a West End café along with Simon Halfon, Gary Crowley, and maybe Eugene Manzi, who worked nearby. Ten to one, Paul would always arrive wearing something new to catch the eye. He was the first person I saw wearing no socks with loafers; the first with white Converse boots, which he wore with bright blue Sta-prest; the first to sling a jumper around his neck; to cut his Levi's jeans into denim shorts; to wear espadrilles; to have his jacket sleeves cuffed; to wear shoes with buckles; to wear a white mac; to wear brightly coloured college scarves; to wear white Levi's jackets and jeans; to wear corduroy shirts; to wear belts of many colours and designs; to wear cardigans with big letters placed on them; to wear a suit jacket with no shirt or vest underneath (he did this at his sister's wedding); to wear granddad tops . . .

It wasn't total emulation – I often wore different coloured boxer shorts – but it gave our little gang an overall look, and psychologically it ensured Paul the control he needed to operate in that environment. He was the Leader of the Look.

What's ironic, of course, is that much of what he was wearing was a copy too. Paul picked up loads of ideas and styles studying pictures from the past. 'You have to know a lot about the old to see the new,' wrote author Arthur Koestler. He might have had Paul in mind when he penned that. I remember in 1981 we gave away a video of music clips with an edition of the *NME*. On it was a rare piece of footage of The Small Faces performing their song All Or Nothing in a Stockholm street. Steve Marriott is wearing his hair centre-parted with a bouffant; he is clean shaven and sports a long corduroy overcoat. Paul saw that clip and soon looked exactly the same in the video shoot for the Jam song Funeral Pyre. He had the haircut and he had the coat. (Paul's obsession with Steve Marriott was such that when I asked Marriott about Paul, he replied, 'I like him. Well, I am bound to, because I like me.')

The Jam style was quintessentially English. They came to life using the Wilko Johnson style of black and white – the same colours in fact in which Paul saw the world. Black mohair suits, white shirts, black ties, black and white shoes. (Paul recently told an interviewer that he had been thinking about those Jam shoes recently and how they should have got a slice of the profits from sales. As this event took place thirty years ago, it tells you much about the man, ruing missed financial opportunities.) In interviews, Weller spoke of Mod and The Who, so in the most uncomfortable photo I have ever seen of him, the band was put in Union Jack-style jackets with ties and white trousers, and snapped at the top of Carnaby Street.

It was when Paul saw that shot and realized how silly he looked that he began to take control of image. Within a year the Jam suits were gone and different colours, different elements came into view. The trousers were always tight, never flared, and rode above the ankle. There were white socks, bowling shoes, polka dot shirts, Prince of Wales check trousers, Lonsdale tops, monkey boots, pork pie hats and corduroy caps, flowered shirts, stripy blazers, Tootal scarves, dark jackets with five buttons on a bunched sleeve, handkerchief in the top pocket, Levi's jeans worn with a half-inch turn-up, red socks, loafers, Harrington jackets. This was the essence of British Mod style.

Then The Jam were gone. New everything required. The first public appearance Paul made after the split was as a guest at the Institute of Contemporary Arts with Tracy Thorn and Ben Watt of Everything But The Girl. Big occasion. 'The thing that most concerned him before we went onstage was what we were going to wear,' Watt recalled. Again, another big occasion, Paul taking part in a Poetry Olympics reading in a large London hall, for the poet Michael Horovitz. 'Can't remember what I read,' Weller once said of this day, 'but I clearly recall the mohair suit and desert boots I had on.'

With The Style Council, the European man emerged. Sunglasses, hair slicked back, striped T-shirts, white raincoat, jumpers tied around the neck. For the photo shoot for their second album, *Our Favourite Shop*, Paul and Mick Talbot brought in suitcases full of stuff that they loved, including pictures, books, records and T-shirts. Paul's favourite item in this mass of cultural iconography? The white belt with SOUL clearly written across it. 'I used to wear it around my head as a kid,' he recalled.

Paul was streets ahead of us. He had the eye and he had the money, but most importantly he was always on the lookout. At a Brighton show, two kids showed up in dark blazers, Madras-style shorts, white socks and loafers. Paul looked down from his position on stage, and that's what he wore for his next photo shoot, a shot for the sleeve of the single. When we went to see the Modern Jazz Quartet play in London, they came on stage with blazers and their own MJQ badge on the top left-hand pockets. The Style Council had similar jackets pretty soon afterwards.

Steve White, the young drummer from Eltham who would prove to be Weller's most enduring musical partner, came to the band with jazz credentials and a bent for South London casual clothes, which also influenced Paul a little. He dabbled in those designer-style wars for a bit, lots of pastel colours turning up in his wardrobe, but the whole point of Paul is never to join the crowd but to move ahead of it, to keep your own thing going.

Into the 1990s, and Paul was spending serious money in the Duffer of St George clothes shop on D'Arblay

Street. What I call a Modhippy look now dominated: the putting together, say, of a simple white top with good shoes and trousers – very Small Faces *circa* 1967. Since 2000, Weller, as befits a man of money and age, has moved more towards a designer style – Prada, Gucci, et al. In the last interview with him that I read (in the *Daily Mail*, of all places), he wore Bottega Veneta shoes ('mega-expensive, but top shoes'), Prada trousers and a green Margaret Howell jumper. As he heads into middle age it's a distinguished look he seems to be cultivating.

Hairwise, different story. Weller has sported a million styles, from short to long, from wedge to feather crop. He looks good in most of them, but sometimes he has badly misjudged things: take, for example, the bleached hair of 1988, or the long floppy fringe he sported in 1985 for the cover of *Our Favourite Shop*, which had us asking him to grow a little moustache so we could call him Adolf. When that album was released, Paul began a tour to support it. In the crowd the night he played the Brixton Academy there must have been a hundred kids wearing Weller's long fringe hairstyle. Lights go down, band announcement is made, and out walks Paul ... sporting a severe crop. A hundred kids' tongues hit the floor, and they were heard to mutter, 'Shit.' 'You'd go to school after *Top of the Pops*,' Mathew Priest of the band Dodgy once recalled, 'and if Weller's hair had changed there would be loads of kids trying to do the fringe, or whatever the new style was.'

One of the last times I saw Paul, his hair was an uneasy mix of yellow and white. 'What the fuck have you done to your hair?' I asked him. He confessed he had just spent £300 on getting it bleached in a King's Road salon. Although time, much to his immense anger and disgust, is robbing Paul of his hair, he refuses to admit defeat and cut it. Like the old man in his song Hung Up, he will keep on going until he reaches his very bitter ends.

FIFTY-EIGHT

I Should Have Been There To Inspire You (*Heavy Soul*, 1997)

Paul and Repentance

Perhaps the best of Paul's 'sorry' songs, and very typical of his attitude when it came to the thorny subject of repentance. Sorry was a word you never really heard fall from Weller's lips. I think he said it to me once, maybe a couple of times, in twenty-six years of friendship. So when he did apologize, the occasion was memorable. As in the time ex-Small Faces keyboard player Ian McLagan played a show at the Jazz Café which I didn't know about and one of my boys, Ronnie Wood, played a guest slot. Paul went but never phoned to see if I was going. When I found out I pulled him up on his thoughtlessness.

'What?' he snapped at me. 'Do I have to tell you about every gig I go to?'

'No,' I replied, 'but a gig like that, Faces people playing . . . put it this way, I would have told you about that show, I would have phoned you.'

Next time we met was at an Italian restaurant in St John's Wood.

'Yeah, sorry about that,' Paul mumbled when I brought the incident up.

And I mean mumbled. Saying sorry did not come easy to Paul Weller. For him it was a sign of weakness, a kind of betrayal of himself. He would rather stand his ground than admit he was wrong. It was only in songs that he was able to express his true view on the matter. There, his thinking tended to follow the same fault lines: I fucked up, everyone around me says I fucked up, but I know better than anyone else that I fucked up. See, what the fools don't know is that I didn't mean to hurt you, and although my friend's words cut harsh and sore, mine will always hurt more. In other words, no one can hurt Paul Weller more than Paul Weller, and there is an undercurrent of sympathy searching that underlines that notion.

Just after his split from Dee, Paul engulfed himself in a haze of alcohol and drugs. His music of the period reflects the way he must have felt about the separation, driven to guilt and desperation over the behaviour that had pushed away his wife and two young children. Perhaps for Paul, this was one way to turn back the tidal wave of emotion that threatened to engulf him and to silence the midnight demons that tore into his soul.

This song is also underpinned by a small conceit,

Paul seeing himself as a source of inspiration for others. He certainly influenced me a little, but never as much as he thought he did. The people who gave me my standards were a diverse bunch: Robert De Niro, Joe Orton, Tony Parsons. I work in a different field. I march to a different drum beat. Musicians, different story. A list of bands and artists Paul has influenced would be lengthy, but they include Oasis, Dr Robert, Carleen Anderson, Ocean Colour Scene, The Libertines, Dodgy, Blur and Billy Bragg. Many acts owe him, just as he owes many acts. That is the nature of the beast.

Funny story. Guy down the road owns a record shop. I go in there a lot. On the release of the eponymous *Ordinary Boys* debut album, people flocked in to buy it. Fuck off, he said to them, buy the real thing, buy The Jam instead. 'I know,' I said, 'but twenty years ago I was walking into record shops and asking for The Jam, and they were saying fuck off, buy the real thing, buy The Who instead.'

This song is hidden away on *Heavy Soul* – last track on side one. Musically, it is a gem, shifting through different shapes and patterns with style and assurance. But unlike John Lennon's Jealous Guy, it lacks one crucial word to really convince. Sorry.

FIFTY-NINE

As You Lean Into The Light
(*Heavy Soul*, 1997)

Paul and Me

One night I got very drunk, very sorry for myself. Suddenly, with no warning at all, my past caught up with me. This is not a good thing to happen, for my past is a horrible place to visit. As a child, I went without love and support; I was beaten physically and verbally. My teenage years were spent in care. As I got older, I began to deal with the loss and the pain, keep them at bay. I was good at it, too, but for some reason, on this particular night, the pain poured out, uncontrollably.

I was with Paul and his partner at the time, Sammi, in a West End bar, and I remember thinking as I spieled out my grievances, 'Shut up, Paolo, just shut up.' But I didn't. I wanted to know the answer to the question that haunts all orphans: why me?

Months later, I went to visit Paul in the Bath studio where he was recording part of the *Heavy Soul* album. He played me this song. I loved its fragile nature, the depth of its emotion. His statement that if he could he would bear the pain of his friend was highly moving.

'Did you like that?' he asked when it was finished.

I replied in the affirmative.

'Good, I'm glad. I really am, because I wrote it after that night. I wrote it about you and that night!'

SIXTY

He's The Keeper (*Heliocentric*, 2000)

Paul and Ronnie Lane

This song is Paul's heartfelt tribute to Small Faces, Faces and solo artist Ronald Frederick Lane. In Paul's world, forces of mysticism surround The Small Faces. Their mix of soul and pop, their eye for clothes, their irreverent attitude and their collective height strike huge chords for him. Although Steve Marriott was the band's main songwriter, the one Paul homed in on and chose to celebrate was actually Ronnie Lane, probably because in the long run Lane produced the better body of work before illness shut off the light inside him far too soon.

Lane has never really been given the critical acclaim the author of songs such as Debris or Just For A Moment should automatically receive. He was an East End boy who wore great clothes and smiled most of his life, thus running counter to the press idea of the great songwriter always being melancholic and ill dressed. Lane once wrote a song, Stone, about the birth of consciousness. If Nick Drake had conceived such a work, *Mojo* would still be running the article on him. Lane still waits for such heavy recognition.

Here, Paul focuses on this injustice: he writes of the man in rusty armour who is so 'undervalued', the man liars and thieves try to buy, the man who hangs wishes on our stars. This is a personal note to Ronnie, crammed full of great imagery and a hurdy-gurdy feel that reflects Lane's time in both the music halls of London and the countryside of Fishpool, near Wales, where he made his home before emigrating to the States to fight multiple sclerosis.

And things didn't end there. From beyond the grave, Lane continued to knock Paul out. Over Christmas in 2003 I took a CD of a live Ronnie Lane concert from Austin, Texas, to Paul's house. When Paul heard Ronnie's song Spiritual Babe on it, he shouted out, 'Rewind!' He must have played that song twenty times. And then another twenty times. The following April, Paul performed Spiritual Babe at the tribute concert for Ronnie at the Royal Albert Hall. A year later, Paul's song Paper Smile appeared with strong lyrical echoes of Lane's composition apparent in lines such as 'What's in a life if you don't live it, baby?'

'I always preferred Ronnie Lane to Rod Stewart,' Weller recently opined. 'His songs were always much more soulful.'

SIXTY-ONE

Frightened (*Heliocentric*, 2000)

Paul and Insecurity

Probably one of Paul's best songs about personal fragility, about the insecure side of his character. Such is the sweeping beauty of this song, so easy is its flow, it really feels as if the music came from above, through Paul naturally. The strings are great as well, designed by Nick Drake's arranger Robert Kirby to swirl and clash to reflect the inner turmoil.

At the time of writing, Paul was living in a large ranch-style house near Woking, complete with non-guitar-shaped swimming pool. The house was set in rolling countryside, and many of his songs from this period reflect the experience: Picking Up Sticks (title taken from a Dave Brubeck tune), Dust And Rocks, Sweet Pea, various lines about black crows, and wheat-fields, and church bells ringing in the distance. He was living alone now, the father of three children, and growing increasingly aware of the unstable nature of his profession. What if he should stumble and fall? How then would he be able to provide for his kin? Such thoughts drive this song, Paul again trying to show the world the truth behind the image: that if that truth be told, he wasn't that bold, he could be as frightened as the rest of us. He also reveals the helplessness he feels at his inability to truly help those close to him, how we all have to stand alone; close friends, yet in truth far from one another, like distant stars.

This song and the other one he wrote on piano for *Heliocentric*, Love-Less, are the stand-outs on an album that some believe to be his finest, the closest to his true artistic side. Yet Paul was scathing about it at the time – a view, I think, coloured by producer Brendan Lynch's fastidious approach to mixing the work. Lynch took about six weeks to deliver, and for Paul that was far too long. Knowing Paul, it was probably a combination of artistic impatience and the budget considerations that drove him to adopt this attitude. At the time of writing, this remains the last album Lynch and Weller worked on together.

SIXTY-TWO

There Is No Drinking (When You Are Dead) (*Heliocentric*, 2000)

Paul and the Demon Alcohol

This song was probably written as a riposte to those concerned about Paul's excessive drinking. Musically it is no great shakes, although at the time it made ripples by echoing the Jam song But I'm Different Now with its chopping Beatles (Dr Robert) style riff. It does, however, make clear Paul's position on the subject of why he drinks so heavily. The thinking is this: who knows what tomorrow will bring? Today is but a second, you may die tomorrow, so enjoy yourself, lose yourself.

Paul started drinking at a very early age. As kids, he and his sister Nicky were taken to their grandmother's every Saturday night while John and Ann Weller went to relax at the local working men's club down the road. Nan would give both children regular sips of her drink. By dint of playing pubs and clubs, Paul began to drink regularly at fourteen. Since then, alcohol has been a consistent factor throughout most of his life. Tellingly, his longest time off the booze began when The Jam disbanded (1982) and continued through the best part of The Style Council's career (1983 to 1985). During this period he wrote some of his best songs. Typically, he now bullishly refers to this time as 'fucking boring'.

Not hard to see why. Alcohol helped to turn a shy, fear-ridden teenager into a confident person. It gave him speedy exhilaration, served to loosen him up, especially when fame first swamped him. Keith Moon's biographer Tony Fletcher, who knew Weller well in his Jam days, made a very perceptive point on this subject. 'Paul only really enjoyed being a pop star when he was drunk,' he once pointed out, and there remains much truth in this statement (see To Be Someone). Paul never used to drink before a show, but in recent years a 'couple of liveners' have helped to loosen the nerves before playing. But he never went too mad at this point. It was afterwards that he would drown himself.

Paul grew up in a drink culture. His father drank a lot, and around Woking there wasn't really much else to do except get into pubs and try to get served as soon as you could. Playing in bands around town allowed Weller this privilege. He learned to drink prodigiously. In the *Flexipop* piece he wrote (see The Modern World), he recalls his parents worrying about him being an alcoholic – and this was in his teenage years.

Yet drink was never really an issue until the nineties when a new hedonism came into play, symbolized by bands such as Oasis and publications such as the highly successful lads' mag *Loaded*. Such was Weller's consumption from this period onwards that everyone close to him at some point came to him and expressed their concern.

Paul brushed off the subject lightly, and then wrote this song.

There are many incidents with Paul where drink is involved. On the night he bumped into Martin Carr from The Boo Radleys, who had consistently made his dislike of Paul known in the press, Paul stood over the seated Carr, castigating him. Later Paul said: 'To be honest with you I was so pissed I can't remember what went on.' (What went on was that Noel Gallagher and I pulled Paul away from Carr and ushered him outside. Paul then tried to get back into the club, but the bouncers were having none of it. Noel saw Paul home. 'Why you stopped me slapping him I'll never know,' was Paul's comment the next day.) On age, his real bugbear: 'I had my sort of crisis last year when I was thirty-nine. I drank my way out of that one.' On the hotel room in Paris that he and his guitarist at the time, Matt Deighton, helped rearrange: 'Drink, I am afraid . . . excessive amounts of booze . . . I was too pissed to remember it.'

On tour, Weller tended to spiral out of control, indulging in lengthy drinking sessions (fifteen hours on one occasion) that saw in the morning sun and sometimes waved goodbye to the evening sun as well. On his return home, he would tell friends he had been 'drinking for England'. He would then take a break from the madness, stay off the hard stuff for a time. But pretty soon he would start up again, by his own admission boozing until every drop in the house had gone.

The fact remains that one of life's greatest pleasures for Paul Weller is getting smashed to pieces and listening to music at a very loud volume.

What kind of drunk was he? That depended on who he was that day or what had happened. Sometimes he was hilarious, brilliant company, witty as hell; other times alcohol seemed to set loose his inner rage, and it was then that he became a mean drunk, offensive and foul-mouthed to everyone around him. Not a pretty sight. Some of the time, both personalities merged into one during a session.

A good example of this would be the night we went to see Brian Wilson play his *Pet Sounds* album at the Festival Hall. There were a few of us in the party: my partner, Paul's sister Nicky, her boyfriend Russ, and Gary Crowley. As soon as we reached the venue, we headed for the bar, downed a few. Wilson then came on and played hits for about an hour. He was absolutely stunning. During the interval we went back to the bar, all of us now fired up by Wilson's music, Paul in particular on good form. Neil Tennant from Pet Shop Boys came over to say hello. (As he approached, Weller whispered to me, 'Here he comes, Neil by mouth . . .') The second half of Wilson's show maintained its incredible musical standard. Probably the best gig I have ever witnessed in my life. It was like watching a modern-day Mozart. I didn't want the music to end.

We left that hall all of us on a huge high. Excitement and wonder tingled through us. The night was too good to stop now. As Paul, Nicky and Gary lived in Maida Vale we headed for a bar there, carried on drinking. We settled at a table. Paul gave Gary money for the first round. He went to the bar, came back to the table with the first set of drinks. Weller misread the situation, thought it was the whole round. Within a flash, he turned on him and killed the mood stone dead.

'Where's my fucking change, Gary?' he demanded.

'I haven't got all the drinks yet,' Crowley explained. 'I'm just paying for them.'

'Make sure you fucking give me the change,' Paul angrily stated.

In an instant the collective mood of happiness had been extinguished. ('If you give me a fresh carnation I will only crush its tender petals . . .') Now everyone was wary. Now no one knew what to expect. Conversation faltered.

Nicky and Russ read the signs. Nicky in particular could see what was coming. One day, returning from tour, she and Paul had shared a cab from the airport. Nicky was sober but Paul was, as he liked to say, 'absolutely rotten'. He handed the driver a CD containing the song Smoke Gets In Your Eyes and demanded he play it again and again and again. When they got to Maida Vale, he even made him drive round their houses in a circle until his lust for the song had been satisfied.

The bar called last orders. Paul seemed to be OK, so Gary suggested going back to his flat, a few yards away. Cigarettes were needed, and there was an all-night garage around the corner. At that garage a girl sat slumped against the wall, begging. Paul saw the girl and straight away sat down beside her.

'What are you doing?' he asked her. 'You shouldn't be doing this, it's wrong.' The girl tried to explain – she had no choice, she was homeless – but Paul kept saying, 'You shouldn't be here, you shouldn't be doing this. It's wrong, it's wrong.' He then pulled out a wad of notes and stuffed them into the girl's hand. 'Go and get yourself a room for the night,' he said, 'and look after yourself.'

The girl looked at the money, amazed. She couldn't stop thanking him. Then she said, 'You know, you really look like Paul Weller.'

Paul replied, 'I know, but don't worry about that, just stop doing this, OK?'

Back at Gary's flat, more drinks. Then Paul noticed Gary's computer. As we know, he hates them with a vengeance. He thinks the internet is the Emperor's new clothing. I don't. I think it's an amazing tool. Paul started coating computers off.

'Fucking internet, load of bollocks . . .'

I'd heard him do this a million times. I started arguing with him. Immediately, the anger returned.

'You want to go outside and talk about it?'

I didn't. I wanted to go home. Which I did.

It had been a typical night. Weller had by turns been funny, charming, generous, obnoxious, threatening, stupefied, unable to walk, and a pain in the arse. On some nights he was just plain funny, but on too many occasions alcohol let loose the volcanic anger inside, and then it was a case of may God have mercy on those in his range.

I can also remember going to see The Zombies with him at a central London venue. He was pissed by the time we got there, only interested in drinking more. I escaped early, so sharp and nasty was his tongue that night. Once, on tour in Italy, his invective pissed me off so much I asked John to get me a flight home. The next day when I told Paul what he had called me, and others, he professed not to remember.

There have been several occasions like this, especially as the years have rolled by. He went to New Orleans, a town whose music both he and I adore. I have always wanted to visit the place, the home of Allen Toussaint, The Meters, Lee Dorsey. I have always wanted to track down their record shops, stock up on their music.

'Did you get any tunes out there?' I eagerly asked him on his return.

'Oh, you know what we're like,' he airily replied. 'We didn't get out of the hotel bar for three days.'

Often Paul and his drinking partners (John, Kenny and Steve Cradock, me at times) didn't even get out of the airport. They would arrive and drink before check-in. On the other side they would then drink again until boarding. Then they would drink on the plane, and on arrival drink at the airport they were in before pouring themselves into taxis. On one occasion he drank so much prior to a flight to Ireland that the authorities wouldn't let him on board. They sent him home, and he had to come back the next day.

One time Paul and his dad were on the lash in Woking. They ended up at the Wheatsheaf pub. The pair went to the bar. Paul ordered the drinks.

'Can serve you, but not your dad,' the barmaid said.

'Why not?' Weller demanded.

'You seen him?'

Paul looked round. His dad had passed out on the floor.

'Just the one, then,' Paul said.

Recently, alcohol has become a test of manhood for Weller. Those unable to keep up the pace are 'pussies, lightweights'. He would say about being on tour, 'It's a man's life in the army.' Those unable to keep up – forget about them. Journalists were a constant source of baiting. 'You lot are rubbish,' he would tell me. 'I did this interview the other day. Four hours in and the guy could hardly walk . . . lightweight!'

If at home alone and he found himself drunk, Paul would often call up friends, sometimes to berate them for some slight, sometimes to tell them that he loved them. He has done both with me. More than likely he would want to play down the phone a track he'd been listening to at full volume which was the 'fucking cunting bollox'. On numerous occasions I have let the phone ring at two in the morning, knowing full well who it is, and what he wants. The next day on the answer machine: 'Oi, Hewitt, check out the fucking drums on this song [holds phone up to a John Coltrane record] ... Fucking amazing! Punk before fucking punk! The cunts! And what is this fucking song you've put on this tape for me? [Drunkenly tries to change tapes, finally succeeds, hits play button.] You're having a laugh, aren't you? Peace out.' And the line goes dead.

Sometimes he would drink himself into such a stupor that you wouldn't even understand what he was saying. The words would come out of his mouth but drop into his chest and just lie there. Often he went into surreal ramblings about cornflakes or toasters, or whatever came to mind. He always had one constant beef, and that was someone who had annoyed him (see Walls Come Tumbling Down) by putting out a crap record or book or film. Or indeed someone just putting out a record, a book, or a film.

When he woke up in the morning and was told of the damage he had caused, the people he had hurt, he would temporarily feel bad. But soon he would tell himself not to worry. Whatever happened the night before was justified. After all, there is no drinking when you are dead . . .

Is he an alcoholic? No answer there, but also no way that man will go to AA if he is one. 'Fucking Christian bollox,' he once said to me about that organization. It wasn't a surprising remark. To enter AA, one has to find humility. Paul, humble? Paul, sitting in a circle with strangers, sharing his experiences? Oh look, four elephants in fur coats have just flown past your window . . . The pride is too big, the craic too enticing. So raise your glass to the big sky, for tomorrow you may die.

Though as the writer Dorothy Parker always pointed out, you rarely do.

SIXTY-THREE

One × One (*Illumination*, 2003)

Paul and the Human Potential

In his book *The Dynamics of Creation*, Anthony Storr suggests that artists sometimes adopt characters through which they then express themselves. The theory certainly resonates when you consider some of Paul's songs. For example, one must hide behind a very wry smile on hearing Paul warn his audience of the dangers of bitterness in Bitterness Rising (*Paul Weller*, 1992) – this from a man who carries resentments as others do loose change. Or when one hears Paul on his unreleased house LP *Decade Of Modernism* (1989) urging the public to love everyone, love everybody in the world. Except, of course, I suppose, Maggie Thatcher, George Michael, Bono . . .

The reason for the power behind this record and its exhortation to the listeners to realize their power and lift their spirits high is that Paul is being absolutely genuine. He really did believe in the potential of all humans, wanted everyone to realize their power in the best ways possible. Paul sensed the bonds, self-inflicted or otherwise, that barred people from making contributions to the world, and in this song he urges his listeners, in a Shelley-like expression, to rid themselves of their chains. In expressing that generous wish he created a great piece of music, almost house-like but somehow not, to make his point even stronger.

He never got this song right in a live setting, but here on the album it radiates a warmth that I find irresistible.

SIXTY-FOUR

All Good Books (*Illumination*, 2003)

Paul and Religion

This understated song shows Paul's religious beliefs finally settling down, making themselves clear. The existence of Jesus or the Prophet Muhammad is not an issue with Paul as such; what is important, what counts, is the message they gave us, and what we do with their words. On previous occasions, Weller has often cried fury at the violence caused by religion, has often denounced its hypocritical nature (see Money Go Round) and railed in private against its practices. Yet here he adopts a more placid tone, almost conversational, which lends greater weight to his argument that we have missed the point of their messages of wisdom and love, that we should be holding dear love and life and not clutching bombs and rifles. Again, Paul does not challenge the existence of God. He knows

326

enough by now to strongly suspect the presence of a higher force at play in our daily lives. What is at issue here is how we use wisdom. Lyrically, he again uses the idea of Jesus being a nearby presence, able to see and hear clearly what we have done with his teachings and the trouble we have wrought. Musically, the song has a recurring structure which, allied to its understated playing, gives it a unique power.

SIXTY-FIVE

Come On Let's Go (*As Is Now*, 2005)

Paul and Now

When Paul first played me this song, my response was, 'Jesus, that sounds just like The Jam.'

'Well,' Paul airily replied, 'if anyone is going to rip The Jam off then I suppose it had better be me.'

And he has ripped them off. The chord structure, I am reliably informed, is the same as, or very close to, the Jam songs When You're Young and That's Entertainment. And fans of Richie Valens may well recognize the title. The very words, in fact, that are inscribed on Signor Valens's grave. Given that, in concert, it is the Jam songs which receive the loudest acclaim, is this Paul trying to rewrite The Jam for the present day? Trying, in fact, to recapture the speed of youth and its daredevil nature? The words are scatter shot, some pertaining to his belief in the oneness of the world ('we are everywhere') and some aimed towards musicians ('sing you little fuckas sing'). This was released as the second single from his *As Is Now* album and was not a great chart success. As the follow-up to From The Floorboards Up, his tribute to the power of his band in a live setting, the song did not reflect the diverse nature of the album, and for many it must have sounded like a man desperate to recapture the past, when youth was on his side and every day was an adventure.

SIXTY-SIX

Pan (*As Is Now*, 2005)

Paul and Musical Direction

When I first heard this unique song, unlike anything the man has ever recorded, I told Paul he should open his album *As Is Now* with it. At the time, he thought it a good idea, but in the end he chickened out. 'Might put people off to open with such a song' was his disappointing argument.

Pan is Paul at his most musical, mixing synthesizers with an almost classical structure. The song sounds natural, not forced, not concerned with anything – money, status – other than creating a fine work of art. The lyrics border on pretentious, but that's good, and the song shows us where this man could go musically if he just put his mind to it. Signs are, however, that he doesn't particularly want to follow that path. 'I like the music I've been doing the past few years and I don't want to change it. Even if I wanted to change I don't know if I have the talent to do so.'

This song argues otherwise, and does so very powerfully.

SIXTY-SEVEN

Savages (*As Is Now*, 2005)

Paul and Politics (Part Three)

Paul's politics had changed enormously since his days in Red Wedge. That experience, and the revelation of the true nature of political life – the space between pragmatism and ideology which can never be bridged – had put Paul off party politics for good.

His dislike had been further strengthened by a growing suspicion of those he felt were simply using musicians for their own ends – good morning, Mayor of London.

British politics had changed too. The Labour Party under Tony Blair had moved to the middle ground, the Tories as well. For most people, Paul included, there is now not much difference between the two. As Noel Gallagher said of Blair, he has destroyed British politics. Paul votes Labour, but only out of a past loyalty. The truth is he thinks as many people do – that all politicians are See You N Ts and out for themselves, not the people. Full stop.

In the writing of this album, Paul's lyrics turned quite introspective. Many of the songs sound as if he is talking to one person, and that person is himself. What exactly is the good news on the song of that title? That he has talent and managed to escape Woking? Who has their head in the clouds in the song Blink And You Will Miss It? Him? A friend? An enemy? Who is old man river after in Roll Along Summer, and why is it such a shame? Is the terse single From The Floorboards Up about his band, those special nights onstage when they and the audience let fly?

Savages suffers from no such confusion. The song shows us that politically Weller has come full circle: once he batted for the left wing and got his fingers burned; now he offers no solutions, he just looks at modern-day atrocities caused by imperialism and fanaticism, and points a warning finger. Such actions have a karmic effect. Do not these savages know that their gods have disowned them? Do they not know that love is coming down to deal with them?

Paul's politics are derived from the spirit now, not the heart or the head.

SIXTY-EIGHT

Left, Right And Centre (Single by Dean Parrish, Written by Paul Weller, Acid Jazz Records, 2006)

Paul and the Future

Cradock, Stephen, born Birmingham, educated Birmingham, guitarist of some repute. When he was growing up, The Jam were Cradock's band. As they did for many like him, working class and music-obsessed, The Jam's acute observational songs about British life hit Cradock in the heart and solar plexus. At seventeen, he was in a band called The Boys. The name was a nod to Weller. In 1978, Weller placed a Boys sticker on the Rickenbacker guitar depicted on the inside cover of the Jam album *All Mod Cons*.

The Boys failed, and several years later another band, Ocean Colour Scene, was formed. Cradock's father Chris, a policeman who couldn't circumvent the freemasons who surrounded him, threw in his badge and began to manage the band. They started to get a name for themselves, and the whispers reached Paul. He took them on tour early in the 1990s, and Cradock was in his element, even more so when Weller asked him to join his band on a part-time basis.

It was a good move. Musically, Cradock understood Paul precisely. He is also a naturally ebullient character, contagious with his energy and smiles, a good contrast to Paul's moodiness. Cradock and Weller liked each other plenty. They emerged from the same culture of music and clothes, scooters and good shoes. Respect existed between the two. Cradock has played on every solo Weller album since *Wild Wood*; Weller has played many times with Ocean Colour Scene. They drew close, as musicians and as friends. They hung out together, visited each other's homes.

When Steve's first child was born, Weller visited him in Birmingham and wetted the baby's head – a little too enthusiastically. Paul came to in Cradock's toilet. They spoke endlessly about co-writing a song. Finally, they went down to Paul's studio in Ripley to see if such a pairing was possible. They ended up allegedly crashed out on Ripley high street at three in the morning, so gone that cars had to swerve around them. Ann Weller rescued them both from the local police.

'Get them home, Ann,' the copper said. 'We wouldn't want this in the papers.'

Cradock would hear no word said against Paul. He defended him fiercely, no matter what. Paul could burn down London and Cradock would make the excuse.

Two years ago, a Jam bootleg surfaced containing recordings from their very early days. One of the songs was a Weller original entitled Left, Right And Centre, recorded in 1976. In musical terms it is a Northern Soul stomper, meaning that a straight-ahead beat drives it forward. The vocal line is catchy, the love lyrics perfunctory, as would befit a seventeen-year-old, and the title is an early indication of Paul's penchant for seizing on familiar phrases.

Cradock contacted the DJ Russ Winstanley and he in turn put him in touch with the singer Dean Parrish. Rick Blackman from Acid Jazz also had the same idea. Parrish is famous in soul circles for a song entitled I'm On My Way, a record that was played last every week at the famous Wigan casino. Parrish came to Britain and the tune was recorded, and released by Acid Jazz Records. It was one of two singles that were released in 2006 with Paul as the songwriter. Wild Blue Yonder was the other, but the less said about that song the better.

It would be easy, so easy, to make use of the fact that the best single Paul Weller released in 2006 was a song he wrote over thirty years ago. That fact might lead us to draw the conclusion that his powers have faded. I think not. In a thirty-year-old career, Weller has proved the world wrong time and time again, so betting against him is a risky option.

Perhaps we should leave the last word to the man

whose view on the matter is now plain and clear. 'It's not a matter of me giving up music,' he recently told the TV cameras, 'it's music giving up on me.'

EPILOGUE

As I think you might have gathered by now, they are different to you and me, the songwriters. Normal rules do not apply. Theirs is another kind of existence, one that moves to a different drum beat. Their moods fluctuate, swiftly. One minute an angel, the next the meanest person alive. They feel themselves special. They are at the centre of the universe, and all because they write three-minute pop songs. Their arrogance is staggering, their humility a sham. They see and feel in different ways.

Kenneth Halliwell, lover and murderer of playwright Joe Orton, once wrote, 'If an artist feels life more deeply than others, should we then not judge them?' I hope this book does not judge Paul. I hope it explains him. I hope it shows the character of the songwriter, that his nature is a common one among those who seek to explain themselves and the world through music. (Obviously I am talking about serious musicians here.) I do not wish to pull anyone up. My position now, after years of pointing the finger, is biblical. Judge not lest ye be judged.

Certainly the very few people kind enough to read the work and offer advice have all said the same thing to me: how the fuck did you put up with him for so long? Good question, but one I hope I have answered already. When the mood takes PW, which it does a lot, he can shine like no other.

But Paul Weller is a handful, and he knows it. He needs no advice from me or anyone else on the subject. When he split up with Gill, I called him.

'Great,' I said, 'we can get a flat together.'

'No, no, no,' he said straight away. 'You don't know what I'm like. I'm impossible to live with. You'll hate me.'

Always stayed with me, that remark. His fear of people changing and leaving him was always very pronounced, and in our case I think that's what happened. We went on a journey and ended up on different roads.

I don't see Paul now. But I hear the stories. Last one I heard had him allegedly drunk in a black cab. The driver looked back and said, 'You're Paul Weller, aintcha? I love your music.'

'Yeah?' Weller replied, belligerence rising. 'If you like my music so much, name me one of my songs and I will sing it to you.'

'Easy,' said the driver. 'You're The Best Thing.'

And so Paul Weller, at forty-eight years of age, sat in the back of a cab and sang one of his old hits to a man who then drove him onwards into the black night.

BIBLIOGRAPHY

The Dynamics of Creation; Anthony Storr; Penguin; 1972

The Jam: A Beat Concerto; Paolo Hewitt; Boxtree Books; 1995

The Jam by Miles; Omnibus Press; 1981

Keeping The Flame; Steve Brookes; Sterling Wholesale Publications; 1996

Mr Cool's Dream: The Complete History of the 'Style Council'; Iain Munn; Wholepoint Publications; 2006

Paul Weller: My Ever Changing Moods; John Reed; Omnibus Press; 1996

All Mod Cons Songbook; 1979

Jamming magazine (various)

PICTURE ACKNOWLEDGEMENTS

PW in Japan, 1982: courtesy the author.

Background: PW and his father, John, backstage at the Empire Pool Wembley, 5 December 1982: Virginia Turbett/Redferns; *clockwise from top left*: PW and PH in a café in Japan, 1982: courtesy the author; The Jam backstage: © Adrian Boot/Retna UK; PW and fan, backstage, Wembley, 5 December 1982: Virginia Turbett/Redferns; The Jam: © Pictorial Press Ltd/Alamy; The Jam on a rooftop, October 1977: © Neal Preston/Corbis; PW and Pete Townshend: © Janette Beckman/Retna Ltd.

Background: PW and PH with Mick Talbot, Paris, 1984: courtesy the author; *clockwise from top left*: PW with Neil Kinnock, Labour Party leader, Ken Livingstone, Billy Bragg, Jimmy Somerville and Frank Chickens (*front*), November, 1985: Getty Images; PW and Bob Geldof, Basing Street Studios, 26 November 1984: Steve Hurrell/Redferns; PW in the mid 80s: © Ray Burmiston/Retna UK; PW,

1985: George Chin/Redferns; PW and Mick Talbot, mid 80s © Patrick Quigly/Retna Ltd; PW and fans in Oxford pub courtyard, 6 October 1984: Getty Images; PW in Paris, 1984: courtesy the author.

Background: PW with Jools Holland on *Later with Jools Holland*: BBC Photo Library; *clockwise from top left*: PW, PH and Johnny Chandler, early 90s: courtesy the author; PW, Glastonbury, 2 August 2007: Mark Shenley/Camera Press; PW and Sammi: courtesy the author; PW and Ray Davies, 16 June 2005: Patrick Catler/Retna UK; PW and Noel Gallagher backstage, 2001: Mark Shenley/Camera Press; PW and Ronnie Wood, Royal Albert Hall, 15 April 2004: Fin Costello/Redferns.

PW backstage at the Royal Albert Hall: © Sarahphotogirl/ Retna UK.

Index

INDEX

INDEX

INDEX

INDEX

doubts over abilities 242
early school gigs 54
fallout with Polydor Records 82, 239–40
and fanzine interviews 66–7
guitar playing 69–70
on his success 137
image and style 22, 23
importance of melody 22
Ivor Novello award 59
knowledge of pop history 26–7, 67
Lifetime Achievement Award 33
love of classical music 238
lyric writing 127, 286
maintaining of high standards 17, 18–19
merchandise surrounding 168–9
and music business 21–2, 79–84, 241
musical influences and tastes 17–18, 24–5, 56–7, 72–3, 93–4, 133, 269–75
and Northern Soul 48
open–door policy for fans 134
and other bands 192–207, 231–2
and press 15, 62–70, 226, 299
and punk 44, 47–8, 80, 126, 247
and recording 187–8
regret theme in work 237
relationship with America 97–8
and r'n'b 232
and romance 190–1, 232–3, 254
search for self knowledge through music 20–1
sets up Riot Stories 137–8, 156
and sixties principles 23
solo career 69, 241–2
songs and adverts 168
and songwriting 15, 18–19, 22–3, 249–53
Spokesman for a Generation label 130
starts Respond label 82–4
status and popularity 89–90
sun symbol in work 173, 237
writing for the piano 238
Personal Life
and alcohol 283, 288–9, 307, 315–24
anger and violence 34, 107–9, 110–12, 149, 246–8
and art 293–5

birth 212
and bisexuality 173–7
characteristics and mannerisms 28, 30–36, 86–7, 98, 114–15, 118, 121–2, 145, 252–3, 298–9
childhood and upbringing 121–2, 150–1, 212, 265
and children 276–8
clothes and hairstyles 297–305
and communication 132–4
confidence of 179–81
and drugs 243, 259, 283, 288–9, 307
and Englishness 97–100
and fame 85–92, 128–31, 182–4
and family 210–18
fascination with passing of time 291–2
favourite books and authors 119, 156–7, 228
fear of happiness 254–5
films liked 119–20
finances 166–72, 215
and friendships 113–23, 290
generosity of 122
girlfriends 51
and humour 30–1, 122–3, 225–7
importance of London to 42–3, 148
influence of mother on 99
and insecurity 313–14
and internet 103–4, 320
isolation in Woking 135–6
marriage to Dee C. Lee and relationship with 231, 254, 268, 279
mood swings 29–30, 32
music collection 26
and nature 173, 257–9
neatness 252
parental background 211–12
and personal freedom 145–6
and poetry 137–41, 156–7, 228–9, 295, 302
and politics 39, 45, 156–60, 222–4, 333–4
property purchases 149, 171, 313
relationship with Brookes 52–60
relationship with father 51, 210–11
relationship with Gill Price 115, 142–4, 174, 230

INDEX